A School for Healing

Studies in the
Postmodern Theory of Education

Joe L. Kincheloe and Shirley R. Steinberg
General Editors

Vol. 105

PETER LANG
New York • Washington, D.C./Baltimore • Boston
Bern • Frankfurt am Main • Berlin • Vienna • Paris

Rosa L. Kennedy
and Jerome H. Morton

A School for Healing

Alternative Strategies for Teaching At-Risk Students

PETER LANG
New York • Washington, D.C./Baltimore • Boston
Bern • Frankfurt am Main • Berlin • Vienna • Paris

Library of Congress Cataloging-in-Publication Data

Kennedy, Rosa L.
A school for healing: alternative strategies for teaching at-risk
students / Rosa L. Kennedy and Jerome H. Morton.
p. cm. — (Counterpoints; vol. 105)
Includes bibliographical references and index.
1. Alternative schools—United States—Case studies. 2. Socially
handicapped youth—Education—United States—Case studies. 3. High
school dropouts—Education— United States—Case studies. I. Morton,
Jerome H. II. Title. III. Series: Counterpoints (New York, N.Y.); vol. 105.
LC46.4.K46   371.04—dc21   98-30629
ISBN 0-8204-4263-1
ISSN 1059-1634

Die Deutsche Bibliothek-CIP-Einheitsaufnahme

Kennedy, Rosa L.:
A school for healing: alternative strategies for teaching at-risk
students / Rosa L. Kennedy and Jerome H. Morton.
–New York; Washington, D.C./Baltimore; Boston; Bern;
Frankfurt am Main; Berlin; Vienna; Paris: Lang.
(Counterpoints; Vol. 105)
ISBN 0-8204-4263-1

Book design and typesetting by Charlotte Duncan
Cover design by Michael E. Kennedy
Cover art © by James M. Kennedy

The paper in this book meets the guidelines for permanence and durability
of the Committee on Production Guidelines for Book Longevity
of the Council of Library Resources.

© 1999 Peter Lang Publishing, Inc., New York

Printed in the United States of America

CONTENTS

PREFACE

O ur time spent working at the school for healing, the Center for Alternative Learning (CAL), was a transforming period. It proved to us what we already knew in our hearts. Our troubled adolescents were caring human beings, who were more positive than negative individuals; and they deserved to be valued by adults. The cause of their troubles was not in their intentions but in the mistakes they made in interpreting the facts of some situations or in the strategies they chose to use to correct injustices they encountered. Thus, our task was not to punish them but to help them learn to interpret situations differently and to use more appropriate strategies to accomplish their goals.

CAL existed before we were involved with it, and it existed after we left it. During its entire history of existence, it has clearly assisted students who have been suspended or expelled from the regular school program. There have been three distinct periods in its history. Each period reflects the use of different combinations of strategies and philosophies for assisting the students. When we were there, we called it the school for healing because of the unique combination of strategies we implemented and our belief system that from each student's perspective he or she had a right to be angry. The student was either misinterpreting the situation or choosing the wrong strategies to resolve a real injustice. None of the strategies or techniques used to assist the students in correcting their mistakes were unique. They have all been tried before and are still being implemented in many schools today. The fact that we combined them in the way that we did and that we interpreted their results through our collective belief system was what made our tenure there a special time. The impact upon the students of this delivery model was very encouraging. It was so positive that the program received the local Chamber of Commerce's Best School Award and the Southern Association of Colleges and Schools' 1990 Exemplary Dropout/Retention Award, was referenced in two books on dropout prevention, had a research article published about it in a national journal, had two doctoral dissertations generated from it, and received other types of recognition.

One of the doctoral dissertations was Rosa's. She did a qualitative research dissertation that conducted and analyzed four in-depth interviews with students who attended CAL, two of whom attended during her employment there. Her dissertation received the 1995 Best Dissertation Award, Division J (qualitative research), from the American Educational Research Association. Her dissertation is the foundation for this book, and the first section is based on that dissertation.

CAL had been in existence for five years before Jerry became its director. The creation of the school took place as a result of a state grant to give high school seniors who had been suspended or expelled from area public schools an opportunity to graduate. It served students from several school systems in and around a midsize city in Tennessee. The school was nonprofit and was controlled by a board of directors. The members of the board of directors were professional educators who had been or were employed by the two largest school systems in the area. They were progressive in their educational thinking. As a budget-saving device, the founding director of the school was employed on a half-time basis. His other work was as a university faculty member.

When Jerry became the next director, CAL had grown to three classrooms serving seventh to twelfth graders. The students came primarily from the area's largest city school system and the surrounding county school system. It was clear that changes in the Tennessee State Department of Education's funding patterns were such that the school would cease to exist in a few years if either a local school system did not take the program over or other funding sources failed to be found. The founding director had left the position to assume a full-time educational administrator's role. During his tenure, he had accumulated a sizable reserve fund for the program. It was decided that the school would expand its service delivery model by supplementing the funding from the two participating school systems with the funds from the reserve. It was hoped that the program could produce more-dramatic positive changes in its students so that a school system or another funding source would step in and continue it. If that did not happen, the school would cease to exist when the reserve fund was depleted. Should a school system decide at some future date to revive CAL, they would at least have a model of a program that was funded well enough to demonstrate that it clearly helped troubled youth.

Jerry saw his new role as director of CAL as an opportunity to put into practice the complete package of ideas he had developed over the years as a school psychologist, an educational consultant, and a director of an educational cooperative. In those roles, he was advising other educators who had responsibilities with school children on how to better assist troubled children. Those educators could accept, modify, or reject his suggestions. As director of CAL, he would have direct responsibility for implementing his concepts for serving troubled youth in an integrated delivery system. By putting into practice his entire set of ideas, he could demonstrate their worth in assisting troubled children and promote their wider acceptance within the educational community.

The key concept that Jerry wished to implement concerned the collective belief system held by the CAL staff about the troubled children they were serving. He wanted the staff to understand that each student operated from a belief that he or she was justified in what he or she did, even though others thought what he or she did was wrong. If they were to have a significant impact in their efforts to assist the child, the staff had to understand how the child interpreted his or her behavior to reflect that he or she was a just and a noble person responding to an injustice. The staff also had to believe that the child was more a positive human being than a negative one and that he or she would respond more successfully to praise than to punishment. In turn, the staff's behavior had to be consistent with these beliefs. The second section of the book describes some of the important strategies used at the school to implement and support the adoption of these concepts.

At the conclusion of Jerry's five-and-one-half years with the program, the newly consolidated metropolitan school system took over the administration of CAL. Jerry was no longer the director. The program changed its focus from a school for healing to providing a second chance for troubled youth to behave appropriately in a more typical educational setting. There was also a need for CAL to increase the number of students it served even though there were no additional funds provided for this extra enrollment. Thus the number of counselors in the program was decreased; and a comparable number of teachers was employed to increase the number of classrooms in the school. There were other management-level changes so that the school as described in this book gradually ceased to exist.

Rosa became involved with the school for healing soon after Jerry became director, and she remained with CAL for a year after the school system assumed administrative control. She is an internationally recognized artist for her pottery creations. Her involvement began as an artist who agreed to volunteer some time to work with a few interested students, and that involvement quickly expanded. Within weeks of her first interaction with students, she enabled them to produce local, regional, and national award-winning paintings. She decided to return to college and become certified as an art teacher while she continued her volunteer work.

CAL received an artist-in-residence grant from the Tennessee Arts Commission, and this enabled Rosa to become a full-time artist in residence. Her role as an artist in residence was different from that of an art teacher in a school setting. She not only provided various art instruction to some students; but, as an artist in residence, she also produced commercially valuable art work at the school. Thus, she was able to demonstrate to students how a commercially successful artist works while encouraging and coaching the students to produce their own art work. She also engaged the region's artist community to do extensive volunteer work and to serve as visiting artists for the school. The sections of the book on the visiting artists and on Rosa's unique approach to assist the students to discover their talents are quite informative (Chapters 9 and 10).

Rosa's increased involvement and the success of her students served as a motivational force for her to pursue her doctorate in education. It was natural that she chose to study the students at CAL and the impact the school had in assisting them to become valued, positive, and successful members of society.

The qualitative research approach of interviewing four representative students at CAL enabled Rosa to bring attention to the affective truths within the young people's lives. These truths are often missed by accountant-oriented evaluations of educational programs. Her interviews of various staff members within the program also add a depth of understanding to what was happening in the program during our years at CAL.

The first part of the book provides the reader with insights into the lives of the troubled students who were suspended or expelled from public school. It helps the reader understand how the adolescents interpreted their negative experiences in the public school setting—how the children can perceive themselves as heroes while their behaviors are seen by the school system and many adults as intolerable. The student narratives were written in the first person as if the students were speaking in the interview. By using this methodology, volumes of extraneous material could be deleted. The indented, smaller type copy represents actual interview statements as supporting evidence to the narrative. The important point to make is that the students' truth was assumed to be the truth. The students' truth is, at times, inconsistent and illogical; but it is their truth.

Then the book explains the various strategies used by the school for healing to help the students be more successful both academically and socially. Rosa's interview technique was also used with the adults working with the children. This approach provides a richness of understanding for the reader that would not be obtained by the descriptive process alone. The last section of the book provides insights to those who are interested in creating a school for healing in their own school systems or communities.

Our experience at CAL provided important lessons. Our assumptions concerning the motivation of the students were correct. They are heroes from their perspectives of their lives. We have to understand how they interpret events if we are to help them become more successful in their culture. The students can and do become enthusiastic learners once they believe in themselves and in the positive intentions of significant adults. Art as an expression of self is an important tool to use in helping the troubled youth understand their uniqueness and the special contributions they can make to society. We verified that positive reinforcement is a better way of working with children to help them change than is punishment—despite the fact that there are always consequences as a result of our behavior and that sometimes those consequences can be negative. We learned that a large number of educators currently working in the school systems can implement the concepts of the school for healing at once if they were given the administrative support and funding to do so. These educators may not be perfect at implementing every strategy, but they do not have to be. All the educators have to do is to keep identifying the behavioral discrepancies between what *they say* they believe and what their *behavior says* they believe. Congruency between beliefs and behaviors is the goal our helping educators, and ourselves, must seek as must we all. The importance of the emotional well-being of the adults who work with troubled youth is another significant point we learned. The staff's good emotional health must be maintained by an administrative support system, or it will be lost—as will much of the positive influence of the program.

We would like to express our appreciation to the host of dedicated educators, artists, and community volunteers with whom we have worked. We find them in all educational settings. We also express the same appreciation to those dedicated educators whom we have never met. You are there working with our children and giving them hope when hope has drained from their faces. However, it is the troubled youth, our boat children, who have been our best teachers. They have had the courage to stand up and protest a system that is not working for them. The fact that much of their protest is misdirected or lacks the skills necessary to be successful does not detract from their courage or their desperation. It is a testimony to the power within them to find a better way. Thanks go to you who have dedicated your lives to helping our children.

PART ONE

How At-Risk Students Describe School

CHAPTER 1

Pam Walker

P am Walker (all names of people, businesses, and locations throughout this book have been changed to protect the privacy of study participants) is white, seventeen years old, and in the twelfth grade. Habitually absent in public high school, during her sophomore year she lost all credit except one unit. She lives with her parents, both of whom had completed high school and some college. The father is a supervisor with Bendix Corporation and her mother is a secretary at a local hospital. Pam worked up to twenty hours per week. From the age of fifteen, she has held several positions with different employers. She reported never using drugs.

Prior to her tenth-grade experience, she had been an excellent student. Her GPA (grade point average) in public school was F when she entered the Center for Alternative Learning (CAL), a private school serving suspended students from public school. Her GPA at CAL when the formal questionnaire was taken was an A or B. Pam was labeled school-phobic, with a major problem of school truancy. She openly voiced her hatred for public high school and for teachers in general. How could an A student become so angered at school and at teachers to allow herself to "flunk out"? She was obviously a capable student. After five months of weekly interviews, I discovered the key event in her life history that led to her feeling that "school is not for me." Here is Pam's story.

STUDENT NARRATIVE

After the Move, School Was Never the Same Again

When I was in the fifth grade, my father got laid off from his job in Detroit. Until then, I was very happy both in school and at home. I went to a private school where I was the center of attention. I did very well—an all-A student. At home I was Daddy's little girl.

Then we moved to Tennessee. I will never forget how awful that first day of school was for me. My parents decided that I should take my fifth-grade end-of-year exams in the new school. I was an outsider and terrified. On that first day, I was called a "Yankee" by the other kids. I got in a fight with another girl who pulled clumps of hair out of my head. School was never the same again. I was always on the outside looking in!

At home too, I was no longer treated in a special way by my father. I guess, looking back, that he was probably busy in his new job. I was only ten years old; I wanted my life to be the same as it was before the move.

> PW: So if I go to my dad, he says, "Go to your mom." I don't see my dad a whole lot. I don't see my dad much. He's gone when I get up. I'm gone when he gets home from work.

For most of my school years, I was still a good student. But I did think the teachers were unfair. They had their favorites, and I was not one of them. I guess what I hated the most was that everyone labels everyone. I got categorized by friends, by teachers, by the company I kept, by the clothes I wore, by what I said, by what I did. See, first I hung out with the Preps. They had rules I didn't agree with. It was really hard to live up to the Preps' standards. I had to have the right boyfriend, he had to have the right car, he had to wear the right clothes along with me, my parents had to have the right profession, I had to say the right things.

> PW: In order to hang (out) with the Preps, I had to put down my own friends. I wasn't going to do that. The Hoods won't judge you by what you have; they will judge you by who you are.

I simply got tired of trying to live up to it. I was trying to be something I am not. I thought it was dishonest. "When I hung out with the Preps, there was no trouble to get into . . . they weren't into getting in trouble!"

In high school it made me feel angry to see students playing up to the teachers for good grades. I called it "kissing butt."

> RK: What about the teachers?
> PW: They have their favorites. The people who kiss butt.
> RK: What about school rules?
> PW: They had lots of rules, but no one ever got caught—no one did anything about it.

RK: Did you have art when you were in school?
PW: I tried to get in, but the classes were full.
RK: Are you a joiner?
PW: No.
RK: Does that bother you?
PW: Sure doesn't, not a bit!

In high school, besides not getting into art class, I couldn't get into Pom Poms or cheerleaders either. I knew the competitions were rigged; I didn't have a chance. The teachers were the judges and everyone knew in advance who would be the chosen ones. Because of knowing how unfair things were, I didn't participate at all.

The Preps and cheerleaders were always chosen as teachers' pets. Because I thought the Preps were uppity, I began making friends with the Hoods. Where the Preps had been exclusive, the Hoods accepted everyone—and they accepted you the way you were, no pretense. I guess switching groups was when the trouble began.

PW: I was friends with everybody—I hung out with Metalheads, Hoods. They taught me how to lay out and not get caught. That's not hard at Jefferson High anyway. I'd lay out (skip school) the first day, and then be sick the second day. Then Mom would write a note. I would sneak out—out all night, meet friends.

I managed that with ease, so I got more brave. My next step was to skip school and hang out at one of the guys' houses during the day, just for fun. I would get back to school in time for my ride home.

Then the Hoods invited me to join them at Brookline Mall at night. I started sneaking out of the house after my parents were asleep. I slipped out the sliding-glass door, leaving it unlocked.

PW: I would say, "I went out to smoke a cigarette" or "I heard something outside"—some stupid excuse, and Mom would accept it. She had no idea! I realize now the rules Mom set for me were in my best interest. Because, she would say, "Pam, anything could happen to you in the middle of the night. Crazies hang out." My mom's from Detroit. Brookton (pseudonym) might not be as bad, but she remembers Detroit. I wanted the Preps to think I was having more fun without them than with them.

I knew I had to be home before 6 a.m. when my dad's alarm went off. A couple of times, I got caught by my mom. I simply lied my way out of it.

PW: Occasionally Mom found out. And then Mom grounded me, but I was already grounded! Mom would get mad—nothing unusual. Brookton's curfew starts at 11 or 12. When they (the police) feel like bugging somebody, they use that! Cop stopped us—called the parents.

When I got picked up by the police downtown after curfew one night, they didn't believe my story about being out to buy a quart of milk for my parents. That's when my parents finally figured out what was going on.

My sophomore year, I received only one credit hour. The pattern was sneak out every night, sick every morning. Both my mom and dad work, so I could stay home alone and have a nice day. Then I would be ready to roam again that night. I was eventually labeled a "school phobic" by a professional counselor. When I was forced to go back to school (because I was threatened with juvenile detention), I really was sick every morning from anxiety, I guess.

CAL was recommended to my parents by my professional counselor. There, everyone was friends because we all knew that we were there because of our problems. We were all in it together. I liked my teacher at CAL a lot. When I first arrived on the scene, my teacher talked to me about a possible law career. She gave me credit for being smart and encouraged me to think of college. But the teacher's aide, I really hated her. She reminded me of my mother. She treated me like I was eight years old. I couldn't stand it!

PW: She (the teacher's aide) said I came in running my mouth, and I didn't say a word when I walked in the door. I walked in the door, sat in my seat, and started doing my algebra. I told Steve [Pam's friend] this morning, "If this keeps up, I'm getting kicked out of here today."
RK: Does she get more demanding when Ms. Hill (the teacher) is away?
PW: She nags!
RK: Does she nag when Ms. Hill is there?
PW: Not so much . . . (mumble). See, if I sit and I work on something else, uh . . . when Ms. Hill is there, I sit right in front of her. If I work on something else, she doesn't care; it's more important. Ms. Zimmer (a substitute teacher) trotted her little butt over to Ms. Fine (the teacher's aide) and said, "Are we supposed to be working on something else when it's journal time?"
RK: Okay, tell me about Ms. Hill (the classroom teacher).
PW: She understands. But Ms. Fine is kind of like a mother—nag, nag, nag! This is what me and Mom would get into. Mom would nag at me and nag at me. And I can't stand nagging. Mom's the kind of person, when she knows you're mad, she'll just keep nagging at you and (it) makes it that much worse. When she starts picking, she don't . . . I would get so mad at my mom that I'd be afraid I'd blow up, would go to my room and she'd

follow.

RK: Tell me more about your mother.

PW: Whatever your parents say, you do just the opposite—something to get you in trouble. . . . The stuff I did wrong, I did to irritate my parents. Mom said, "Why do you ask my opinion? You know everything, anyway."

NARRATIVE DISCUSSION

Pam was the first interviewee in the research project. From her story, I gained insight into how to proceed with further interviews. As a means of sorting information, I searched for a "key event" or turning point in each story. In Pam's case, this was easy: The move from Michigan to Tennessee, from a northern culture to a southern culture, was pivotal. As I listened to Pam speak about events in her retrospective life history, some details were passed over lightly while others were discussed as though she were describing a video movie. I believed that many of those highly descriptive events had been stored in her visual memory and that much of her meaning perspective was based on how she interpreted those events. I labeled those highly descriptive events that seemed to "replay" over and over again as significant material "visual overlays."

The student's action, labeled "outcome," is based on his or her visual overlay of key events. A three-part model for excluding many hours of extraneous interview information and for creating a structure parallel to other interviewee information became: *key event—visual overlay— outcome*. The principle here is that the way in which we interpret and remember events affects the outcome by the choices we make. This model worked well for sorting data from the three other dropouts/pushouts whose stories follow.

In looking at Pam's meaning perspective change from one of liking school to one of hating school, I wanted to know if that hatred was tied to any past events. The label of school phobic and the process it takes for a student to acquire a label like that aroused my curiosity. Pam Walker did not fit the criteria of low SES (socioeconomic status), of being a minority, of coming from a broken home, of having parents who did not support the educational process, of being a poor student, of being language deficient, and other variables researchers use to predict dropping out. I learned in the process that some dropouts were actually pushouts, that schools simply were not willing to accommodate some of the difficult students. I also knew by reading *What Anthropologists Have to Say About Dropouts* (Trueba,

Spindler, & Spindler, 1989) that the "native" or emic point of view (the meaning perspective of the dropout) had rarely been considered by educators. This study began as an attempt to understand more about the perspectives of students who dropped out or were pushed out of schools.

Six months of regularly interviewing Pam identified the family move as a key event. Pam wanted to express her hatred of school by telling me every ugly story about school, about teachers, about peers, and about family members. Volumes of hard copy, transcribed from taped interviews, became extraneous material after the three-part model was created.

In Michigan, Pam had attended a private school. She was an excellent student and a favorite of teachers. The reason for the change from private school in Michigan to public school in Tennessee may have been due to the father's loss of income. They appear to have enjoyed an affluent lifestyle in Michigan. Another reason may have been the time frame of the move, which occurred near the end of the school year. To enter the major private high school in Brookton, a student must be tested well in advance of school entry to prove a high academic capability.

After the move, the family dynamics changed radically. It appears that Pam's father became so involved with his new work that he gave little attention to Pam, who, up to this time, had been "Daddy's little girl." It seems that Pam's father became aloof and that her mother took over the role of primary parent. Pam described her mother as not dealing well with the stress of moving. After the move, her mother sometimes borrowed money from Pam in order to go on major spending sprees. Pam said she decided then that she would never "live like that" (without enough money for what she wanted). As soon as Pam was able to work, she always had afterschool jobs. Pam noted humorously and sarcastically, "No trouble getting to work on time, only trouble getting to school on time. Can't get fired from school!"

Money was a symbol that aroused anger for Pam. While I tried to understand Pam's meaning system about money, I remained confused. Tied to her values about money were the concepts of (a) Preps, (b) labels, (c) wasteful spending, (d) allowances, and (e) father–daughter relationships. Examples from Pam's interviews illustrate her understanding of these concepts.

The concept of money triggered memories of Preps being given daily allowances by their fathers. She described a young female friend in a frenzy to spend that day's allowance so that her father would give her more money the next day. Her narrative included words like "the right house, the right car, the right clothes." Pam also described wasteful spending that reminded her of how her mother acted directly after the move.

Money also triggered memories of how her female friends used clothes to compete for boys' attention in a competition that obviously angered her. She described inviting one friend to meet her at the mall and the anger she felt because her friend was so dressed up! Pam spoke about clothes as status symbols and competition. Pam felt that teachers were more likely to give positive evaluations to students possessing the "right" material goods. It angered her that teachers played favorites according to student status derived from family income.

During the interviewing process, Pam referred to "before the move" and "after the move" in discussing many different subject areas. One was the way in which her mother dealt with the stress of the move; another was the difference at school; still another was Pam's experience with the Preps, who flashed their money and purchasing power in front of their peers in order to maintain their position.

Pam aspired to be a Prep but was never accepted in the circle. It appeared that both at school and in her family she experienced alienation. In high school, she tried out for Pom Poms and refused to try out for cheerleader, saying that the competitions were rigged so that teacher favorites were the winners. It was obvious to her that she was not a teacher favorite.

From Pam's description, one would assume that there were only two peer groups with which to associate in her high school. She called the Preps dishonest, pointing out that they were acting out the status game of wealth. The other group, called both Hoods and Metalheads, accepted people for who they were without judgment. She never described them as "druggies," nor did she include anything negative in her description.

Once Pam made the choice of identifying with the Hoods, her meaning perspective about school had to change. The Hoods were antischool. The Preps were proschool. With Pam's association with the Hoods came the beginning of her truancy. She described a learning process, a peer group socialization process, whereby the Hoods taught her how to skip school and not get caught. Instead of putting forth effort to pass her academic subjects, her focus became how to outsmart school authorities, beginning with the "cop" in the school parking lot. She said that she felt very smart for laying out of school and not getting caught. It appears that she did not consider the long-term effects of truancy.

Beating the system became Pam's challenge instead of achieving success in school. The Hoods had daytime gathering places and nighttime gathering places. In order to spend time with her new friends, she began sneaking out of the house at night. She was forced to lie to her mother on several occasions to cover her tracks. This dishonesty was a drastic change in Pam's meaning perspective. After all, it was because the Preps were dishonest that she chose to join the Hoods.

Pam's willingness to accept failure in school paralleled her desire to belong. Sneaking out of the house at night left her with no desire to attend school in the daytime. She feigned illness for so long that she became ill at the thought of school.

Pam's symbols of interaction became antischool, antiteacher, anticop, antiparent, anti-Prep, and antimen. She described men as "pigs" because of perceived sexual harassment to herself and favoritism shown to men in the workplace. Her attitude toward men did not fit the picture as closely as the antischool, antiteacher mind-set. It may be that Pam perceived men to be authority figures, and she was definitely antiauthority figure.

The issues of Preps as the moneyed class, her mother's misuse of family funds as a stress release, her friend's need to look better than Pam when they went to the mall, and teacher favoritism were richly described in the interviews. They appear to have connections to one another in Pam's storage of symbols in memory. She justified her choices according to how she interpreted others' actions.

Pam liked CAL. She said that students there all leaned on each other because they all knew they were there because of problems. Ironically, Pam acted like a Prep at CAL. She was described by a staff member as "Barbie-doll cute, fashionable clothes, not looking the part of a dropout." She was one of very few who had her own car. She said she never thought about the Hoods anymore. Never gave them a thought. The reason she gave was that her mother no longer grounded her.

Pam's interviews revealed that hers was a classic example of individuals described in anomie theory (Merton, 1957). Anomie means misfit. Because Pam's culture changed dramatically due to the move, Pam's social code and value norms, as learned in the private school of the North, were different from the new group consensus. Pam was not from an established southern family. She brought the symbolism of the North with her in the form of dialect, dress, a desire to be popular, and a desire for a college education. The institutional methods of the southern schools were tied to the southern cultural norms, which Pam did not understand. Pam no longer had full and equal access to opportunities.

According to Merton's (1957) axiom, genuine failure leads to a lessening or withdrawal of ambition. "When the institutional system is regarded as the barrier to the satisfaction of legitimized goals, the stage is set for rebellion as an adaptive response" (p. 156). For Pam, the acute dissonance between cultural norms imported from a private school in the North and the barriers set up by the public institution of school in the South provided a rationale for Pam's later decision to join the Hoods, who accepted her as an insider.

Acute anomie is marked by a deterioration of value systems, or in the extreme, by the disintegration of value systems, marked by anxieties. When Pam joined the Hoods in order to become an insider somewhere, she was forced to accept a meaning system very different from the one she brought from the North. For acceptance in the Hoods, she gave up her valuing of education, of regular attendance in school, of good grades, and her acceptance of authority figures—both teachers and parents. In order to satisfy her immediate need to belong and feel loved, she gave up her long-term goal of attending college. Her immediate goals, adapted from the peer-group culture of the Hoods, were to "beat the system" by practicing truancy and not getting caught. This gave Pam the feeling of "power," one of the five basic needs stated by Glasser (1986).

> If their friends work hard in school, then they, as the haves, will be motivated to work hard to keep these friends. But if they are friends with the have-nots and those friends are dissatisfied with school as they are, their friendship is strengthened by the fact that they all hate school. (p. 11)

The five basic human needs as described by Glasser (1986) are to survive and reproduce, to belong and love, to gain power, to be free, and to have fun (p. 23). An assumption of Glasser's control theory is that our actions and interactions are initiated by "satisfying pictures of that activity that we store in our heads as a pleasant memory" (p. 34). Glasser believes that the at-risk student's positive mental image is replaced by

> . . . pictures of themselves rebelling or withdrawing. What students do in school [and out] is completely determined by the pictures in their heads. (p. 39)

> Starting immediately after birth, instructed by our feelings, we begin to learn what is satisfying and what is not. We learn almost all that we know through parental teaching. . . . . When we learn anything that satisfies one or more of our needs, we use all of our developing senses like a multisensory camera and take a picture of this need-satisfying situation. . . . We keep only those pictures that are in some way need satisfying to us. (p. 35)

In joining the Hoods, Pam satisfied two of the other basic human needs besides the need for power: the need to have freedom and the need to have fun. When Pam skipped school, part of the fun was to see if she could leave school and not get caught. At first she went to a boy's house within the neighborhood where parties gathered. Later she began sneaking out of the house at night to attend gatherings at Brookline Mall. "If they are lonely, they will spend their time looking for friends rather than knowledge," says Glasser (1986, p. 15).

Pam was not only lonely at school but lonely within her own family. She had been "Daddy's little girl" when she attended private school in the North. Her father's loss of employment in Detroit initiated the move to the new location and a possible lowering of social status. The highly descriptive material from the transcript connected with the move were issues surrounding money, teacher favoritism, and workplace favoritism. Her mother's spending spree after the move appeared to be related to Pam's observation of southern girls accepting generous allowances from their fathers. This visual overlay appeared to be connected with teacher favoritism, cheerleading competitions, and male chauvinism in the workplace. Pam had a lot of anger about everyday life that appeared to come from the social context. Her value-system change was likely derived from membership in the Hoods. Glasser (1986) writes that "All of our behavior, simple to complex, is our best attempt to control ourselves to satisfy our needs, but, of course controlling ourselves is almost always related to our constant attempts to control what goes on around us" (p. 17).

When human needs are defined as sex, love, power, freedom, and fun, Pam Walker's behavior becomes acceptable and understandable. From the educator's point of view, however, Pam was perceived to be sick or maladjusted (school phobic) and at risk of dropping out—even though she was academically capable of high school graduation and college entrance.

CHAPTER 2

D. J. Whitebear

D. J. Whitebear was chosen as a participant for this study because of a poem he had written about his personal life history. During the interview process, I learned how his relationships at home affected his school behavior. D. J.'s poem follows:

Born in Mercy Hospital
In Brookton, Tennessee.
Mom and Dad together then
Till the age of three.

Lived in Californ-i-a
Dad came then, stole me away.
Age of six to New Orleans
Mom then drank and spilled her beans.

Got a place in Blueberry Plains,
Moving fast and changing lanes.
The fighting of parents was getting bad;
The son, the daughter were feeling sad.

Exchanges of children to and fro—
It's time for me, I have to go.

Drinking booze, it ruled her then;
My Mom began to date the men.
It seemed to me, she was in sin;
I felt I had no chance to win.

Stepdad and alcohol sure don't mix.
At an early age, they provided the fix.

Yes, it was fun, I do admit.
The fighting made my life worth shit.
It's time for me, I have to go.

I took a knife and willed it so.

But life went on, day-by-day.
I knew by then I must change my ways.

At grandmother's house, it was cool.
I had my freedom, yet I had my rules.
I broke some rules, but I was fine.
Nothing could stop me, the world was mine.
I realized what it means to be alive.
It's not worth it, you see, I mean to die!

My Mom has calmed down a lot,
No more booze and no more pot.
My life is together now it seems.
Now I'm reaching for my dreams.

And for me, art is the way
I'll express myself each and every day.
Paint and canvas; college too—
The future is bright for me and you.

D. J. was nineteen at the time of the interview. He was in the tenth grade when he walked away from public high school. He had long blond hair and appeared both shy and sensitive. He described himself as a loner. He was slight in build, medium height, and quite thin. It was common knowledge at school that D. J. lived with his father in a log cabin with no running water. D. J. worked, cleaning office spaces at night. His father expected D. J. to give him all of his money for car payments and later for trailer payments.

STUDENT NARRATIVE

Drugs were part of my family life. My mom is my best friend.
My mom, she's an alcoholic for as long as I can remember.

I was told that as a newborn infant, my mom blew marijuana smoke through a straw into my face to calm me down and stop my crying. Ironic, isn't it, that most of my problems in school have been over smoking or drugs?

I didn't understand, when I first went to school, why there were rules against smoking.

DJ: I remember the first time I was smoking; it was in the third grade and I would come home everyday and my mom and I would smoke and watch cartoons and stuff and then I had to get in the shower before my dad got home. But . . .

RK: So your mother is the first one to give you pot?

DJ: As far as I can remember . . . they say I did it when I was in the crib to help me go to sleep. I don't know.

RK: She would do it through a straw?

DJ: Yeah, my mom said my dad did it and my dad said my mom did it. I know my dad didn't do it because I used to have to take a shower and put eye drops in so (pause) so I know it was my mom. It was my mom. [D. J.'s mother was trying to remove the evidence of D. J.'s marijuana smoking.]

My favorite time was smoking pot and watching cartoons. I must have been eight years old. My worst time was being hunkered down in a corner with my arms up over my head, protecting myself from family fights— fights between my mom and dad. When things were really bad, I would run away to the woods by my house and sometimes stay overnight. A friend and I lit a fire contained by a tire one time, and I had to get my mom to help put the fire out.

I hate fights. I always want people to get along well with each other and to show some kindness for one another. One of my early memories is of watching my dad hold a gun to my mom's head and threaten her while she was brushing her hair in front of the mirror. Neither she nor I knew whether the gun was loaded or not. My dad held the gun at her temple so she could see it in the mirror. He said, "This could kill you anytime."

DJ: In my family everybody hates everybody. Everybody is always talking about everybody. Putting down each other. Everybody is better than everybody else.

At first my parents fought over who would get me because they wanted me. Now they fight over who gets me because no one wants me.

When I was quite young, five or six, my mom and I moved to California. I can just barely remember school there. It was pretty good. The playground was on the beach and I used to mess around with the girls. That was a pretty happy time.

My dad came on my sixth birthday to bring me back to Tennessee.

DJ: Brought me and my mom back. What I heard was . . . what my mamaw [grandmother] says was that the reason my mom got married back with him [remarried after divorce] was because he broke into a pharmacy and he was looking to go to jail, so she came back with him to marry him to keep him out of jail. That is what mamaw says.

My mom has had it rough. . . . She's been an alcoholic for as long as I can remember. Both my dad and my stepdad threaten her, smack her silly. One time I stood up for her against my stepdad. That's when I got kicked out of the house.

DJ: This was why I left my mom's house. Because . . . so I was taking up for my mom and then she said, "You are going to have to find somewhere else to live. We can't put up with you anymore." I was thinking it was partially because they could not afford to keep their drinking habit up and keep me too. But they said it was because I told my mom "F--- you," that is not a very good reason because I was taking up for her. She is still in the same situation—same situation. Now she can't . . . every time she tries to get a bite to eat she pukes. She can't eat. She has voices in her head.

Maybe "being between my mom, my dad, and my grandmother; and my other grandmother; and all around in a circle," maybe that affected my time at school. I was first in school in Tennessee, then in New Orleans and California, and then back to Tennessee. I went to Creston, Madison, Oakview Middle, Madison, Jefferson, and CAL (two different times). But I thought nothing really bothered me about all the school moves.

I always had trouble with math; I was held back in the third grade— given a social pass. But all my problems in school had to do with smoking or having pot or whiteout on me. I never blamed teachers or school for that. (Whiteout is correction fluid used to cover typing errors. Students sniff the fluid to get high.)

Teachers do play favorites with Preps and Jocks and that sort. In one math class, I noticed that Jocks never attended but still passed. Of course the math teacher was a coach! I figured maybe the Jocks were smart enough to pass the tests without having to study much. Maybe they were smart in math. That never bothered me even though I heard other kids talking about it. What did bother me was that most teachers didn't like people with long hair. And I always had long hair! They just stereotype, I guess.

When I finally walked away from school, it was because I wouldn't fight the punks at Madison. They chase you around everywhere and try to beat you up.

DJ: Like one time at Madison this big old black guy, his dad taught martial arts, and he was a black belt and he just came up to me and said, "I heard you were in my locker." I said, "Where is your locker?" He pointed right behind me and said, "Right there." I looked around and turned back around and he had all these rings and went "pow" and I turned around and he hit me in the back of the head and I got up. And the office was about from here to there [pointing], and I said [to myself] you are not worth me going to Juvenile over. I told on him; but he was a football guy, and they were in favor of him, you know; and they didn't want to suspend either one of us.

I just started laying out because I didn't want to fight. I thought if I reported the incident that I would be the one to end up in Juvenile. And the punk simply wasn't worth that. No one ever called my dad about the cuts because we didn't have a phone.

RK: So nobody ever tracked you to find out why you were not at school? You could just walk out the door and that was the end of it, and nobody ever said anything?
DJ: Yeah, they never did bother me.
RK: What grade were you in when you left?
DJ: Tenth or eleventh. I don't know.

My dad didn't care whether I went to school or not. He thought I should be working to help him make trailer payments and pay room and board to help him out. He doesn't want me to go away to school, but I guess it would be all right with him if I go to college locally. He doesn't value education like my mom does.

I never blamed the schools for my problems, except maybe for not stopping the fights. I never saw any fights at CAL. Things were different there. I did my work there, but I always had help. I thought the teachers there were my friends and that they wanted me to succeed. I believe I would have graduated regular rather than getting a GED if they would only have let me finish there. But they were good about explaining why they needed to send me back to regular school. I just couldn't fight. My dad blamed me for not fighting, but I just couldn't fight.

NARRATIVE DISCUSSION

For D. J., the key event was being born into a household where drug and alcohol use and abuse were acceptable behavior. After his parents divorced a second time, no one wanted him, including his grandparents.

D. J.'s best memory is of coming home from school to watch cartoons and to smoke pot with his mom. D. J.'s worst memory is of protecting his head and body while his parents fought. His mother is his best friend; and yet, his mother has been an alcoholic for as long as he can remember. What appear to be inconsistencies to an outsider seem to be integrated in D. J.'s meaning system as child perception versus adult perception. Both realities are the "truth" for this participant.

D. J.'s reasons for leaving school were school fights and threats of fights. He was already in trouble with the court system because of drug charges and needed to keep his record clean. Besides, no principal would take his word over the word of one of the Jocks. During member check, when the participant reads the story as written by the researcher, D. J. said that, in fact, he did report the incident to the principal, who chose to do nothing about it. The Jock was well respected at school, and D. J. was labeled "deviant" if not a "dropout." Once negative labels are attached to a student, even unofficially, the labels are rarely forgotten. Even if the student makes major changes through programs like CAL, the public schools continue to treat the student according to previous labels.

D. J. expected stereotyping by teachers, especially over his long hair. He expected to be treated like a druggie because of his several expulsions from school for possession of illegal substances. He did not participate in school activities, wishing only to get through the day so he could go home. But the location of "home" frequently changed for him. Sometimes he lived with his mother and stepfather. Sometimes he lived with one grandmother and then with the other grandmother. Sometimes he lived with his father. He had problems with both his father and his stepfather, both of whom, D.J. felt, abused his mother. His father thought D. J. should quit school and go to work. His mother always supported D. J.'s staying in school. D. J.'s perception was that his mother could not afford to support him and her alcoholism too. His stepfather was also a heavy drinker.

As D. J. spoke about his mother, his conflict about how to represent her was evident. The symbols of good mother as best friend and bad mother as alcoholic were in direct opposition. Because of D. J.'s experience of the negative effects of alcoholism due to his mother's problem, he believed alcohol to be highly destructive to one's health. It took D. J. a long time to believe that marijuana and other drugs were detrimental as well.

When the school expelled him for smoking cigarettes, something he accepted as normal behavior, he was rejected again—this time by his social group rather than by his family. His experiences at school promoted the low self-esteem syndrome begun at home. D. J's meaning system contained many conflicts: substance abuse as comfort versus substance abuse as crime; family norms versus school rules; alcoholic mother versus mother as best friend; father as exploiter of D. J.'s earning capacity versus father as supportive parent.

Two important points are evident. First, D. J. and others like him are described in the academic literature as passive learners, disengaged from classroom pedagogy. In fact, at times students are not able to concentrate because of worries about home. D. J.'s poor academic record was often labeled as a result of boredom when in fact there were more important issues for him to deal with in terms of his personal survival. His nonparticipation in school activities was another risk factor as pinpointed by Kronick and Hargis (1990). In fact, D. J.'s nonparticipation had more to do with lack of parental support for school and lack of transportation for after-school events.

A second point is that educators too often assume that students have parental support about education. We also assume that the student's home life resembles our own. More and more, educators must face issues of trauma within the family unit and the lack of parental support for school attendance. When students are from low SES (no running water, no phone, sometimes no electricity), they have little status at school where white, middle-class standards prevail.

D. J. couldn't change his family; and he couldn't change his addiction to nicotine, even though he tried. He experienced some success at both Jefferson High and at CAL but was continuously getting caught with illegal substances at school. He had trouble believing that carrying a pack of cigarettes to school was cause for expulsion. He believed smoking to be acceptable, normal behavior. He never understood why there should be a school rule against smoking. As an addicted smoker, he sometimes got the "jitters" in the classroom and needed a cigarette to be able to settle down to learn.

D. J. chose to leave school. He did not blame the school system for his failure, even when they did not follow up on his absences. He rationalized this by explaining that his father didn't have a phone. D. J.'s school district does not track students who are labeled troublemakers when they leave school. The school's meaning perspective appears to be "Good riddance!"

D. J. was never rebellious, as Pam Walker had been, even though he, too, perceived himself to be a loner and a misfit. D. J. fits in Merton's (1957, p. 140) scheme as a "retreatist"—one who has abandoned both the once-valued cultural goals of getting ahead by means of education and the institutionalized practices directed toward those goals.

D. J.'s choice of retreatist behavior in school paralleled his retreat to the woods as a young boy when his father and mother were fighting. His past experiences of seeing his father hold a gun that might have been loaded to his mother's head, and witnessing the physical abuse of his mother by both his father and his stepfather induced D. J. to create positive fantasy images that everyone in his family was able to get along with each other. Glasser (1986) has described the process of replacing negative visual images with positive images. He states that as a person interprets events as either positive or negative, that the negative events are gradually forgotten and replaced by positive mental images. These self-pictures can change as student self-concept evolves.

Little research has been conducted on retreatist behavior, since the behavior is passive and does not create problems within the classroom in terms of disruption of teaching time. Merton (1957), however, did describe this social response as being identified with "problem families," which were described as those families who do not "measure up to the normative expectations prevailing in their social environment" (p. 187).

When I asked D. J. about early school experiences that had created academic obstacles for him, he interrupted my question to say, *"I guess, problems at home. I had them in my head at school"* (emphasis mine). He went on to say that there was nothing he could do about the problems at home when he was in the fourth grade. His solution was that of a young child: "Went to the woods and stayed in the woods." I asked him, "Was that on the weekend or were you cutting school in the fourth grade?" D. J. said, "I think I was cutting school." Cutting school in the fourth grade with no adverse consequences paralleled later retreatist behavior when problems arose at school.

In discussing the labeling of deviant behavior, Schur (1971) described rule changes that compel a person who is socially acceptable in one group (D. J.'s family) to be labeled deviant by another group (school authorities). D. J. was raised to believe that smoking pot was a normal and perfectly acceptable behavior. He openly stated that he did not know that smoking of any kind was against school rules. "I never thought there was anything wrong with it (smoking pot). I was brought up, there wasn't anything wrong with it." D. J.'s mother and father both smoked pot regularly during his early childhood.

While Glasser (1986) speaks of basic needs beyond survival, it appeared that at times D. J. was concerned with survival itself. His visual overlay of protecting his head during fights was real to him. His reason for walking out of school and never returning was because of the threat of physical violence by a fellow classmate.

D. J. described satisfying his basic need to belong by smoking pot with his friends at Jefferson High. "Me and Michael and all of us would smoke pot sometimes in the morning over at Glacial Springs and then walk over to auto mechanics. It was fun." He spoke of being expelled for smoking as "three days of freedom." This correlates with Glasser's (1986) basic-needs list for freedom, fun, and a sense of belonging.

Freedom and fun were threatened continuously by school authorities who had rules that dictated nonsmoking as an institutional policy. D. J. chose friends at school who smoked pot. D. J.'s interest in school was aligned more strongly with smoking pot with friends in the back lot as symbolic interaction than with the long-term goal of getting an education in order to gain power. The short-term need to have fun with friends was stronger than any long-term need to gain an education.

Students like D. J. generally do fairly well in elementary schools in which there are self-contained classes with caring teachers. D. J.'s positive memory of early school, however, was described as a recess situation in which he played with his friends on the beach in California. In junior high school, teachers became less available and less personal. For D. J., with all of his family issues, school became less and less a place where he felt a sense of belonging. D. J. did not even have his father's support to remain in school.

> If they [the students] flunk and feel powerless, they . . . use drugs, mostly alcohol, to try to gain the feeling that they have some power. If no one respects them, drugs give them the feeling of power and respect that they desperately want. (Glasser, 1986, p. 15)

As schoolwork became more difficult, smoking pot or skipping school became more fun; and that was D. J.'s choice. "Teachers are well aware that hungry students think of food, lonely students look for friends, and powerless students for attention far more than they look for knowledge" (Glasser, 1986, p. 20). D. J. was a lonely student who felt a sense of belonging when he was smoking pot with others.

Glasser (1986) stated that negative images are dismissed and that positive images control our choices for behavior. D. J. chose marijuana rather than alcohol. His image of alcohol use was that of his mother unable to keep food down during her binges and having to cope with "voices in her head." D. J. smoked pot but chose not to drink alcohol.

A major question to be asked after reading this case study is: Should schools expel students for breaking the rules? If, in fact, expulsion from school is perceived by the deviant as three days of fun and freedom, then are we not missing the point? Sometimes the breaking of rules by a student is a cry for help. Should there not be someone within the school to begin to ask the right questions in order to give the student some insight into his or her choice of behavior?

But it is always the difference between the pictures in our head and the situation in the world that starts us misbehaving. A student may have to behave defiantly so he or she can get expelled from school in order to gain control of his or her life. If there is no visual of satisfying any personal need by learning in school, learning will not take place simply because a teacher demands that a student learn (Glasser, 1986).

CHAPTER 3

Iesha Wilson

Iesha Wilson was violent and unruly in public school. She was enculturated by a social group that practiced violent behavior; her early childhood experiences affected her choice of behavior that was considered deviant by the school. The behavioral norms in the West Brookton Middle School, to which she was transferred because of integration policies, and the norms in her neighborhood elementary school were in opposition to each other. She chose rebellious behavior as her way of acting out her feelings of being a "misfit" in the new school environment (Merton, 1957)

At the time of the study, Iesha was a fourteen-year-old African American girl who lived in the housing projects. Her family was on welfare. She had nicely styled jet-black hair, sparkling black eyes, light-brown skin, and a small gold leaf in her left nostril. She was of average height and size. She was highly verbal, telling her stories with the visual details of an artist. She had many stories to tell that shocked me; this may have been responsible for the easy relationship we enjoyed. She was a storyteller, and I was her audience.

STUDENT NARRATIVE

Violence Is Where the Action Is

You (Rosa Kennedy) may have played with Barbie dolls for your fun, but I want to be where the action is. I love violence!

RK: So how many times did you see that [shootings] happen in the projects?

IW: I seen, I seen at least twenty-five people shot. And I seen about six people die.

RK: Do you think it was all drug related? Or were there—

IW: Well, most of them were all different reasons. I seen my sister's boyfriend die because some guys called him "nigger," and they started fighting and some guy just broke out with a gun and started shooting. Then . . .

RK: What was the first fight in school that you got in trouble for?

IW: It was in the fifth grade. This girl called me out by name and talking about my uncle. And my uncle had died that year. He had got killed. And she said, "Your uncle stinks and your mother smells. Your mother went to heaven and your uncle went to hell." And it just got to me. I just grabbed her hair and rammed her head into a brick wall, and I got in trouble for it. All they did was suspend me for fifteen days.

I watched as my sister's boyfriend got shot in the stomach. I watched as some of my friends found a dead body in this guy's backyard.

RK: In the yard you mean?

IW: No, it was in an electrical box. And I seen them pulling that body out of that electrical box, and I seen it when it [the body] was in there and the man had been beat, had big old gashes out of his head. It looked like someone had broke baseball bats on him, it looked like someone took a whip and whipped his back, it was all these slashes all over his back. He was not blue, he was not green, he was red. And he had been there for like a day and a half. And his mom. . . . his brother had got killed two days before they found his body.

During a drug deal, I saw another man get splattered against a Dumpster. The police came and drew the chalk line around the splattered remains of the body so that we, in the neighborhood, were reminded of the killing every day until the weather finally washed the chalk away.

IW: Well, this guy named Ricardo, he had just got a new gun; a sawed-off shotgun, and he shot the guy in the back of the head. And he fell in the middle of the street, but it was like the Dumpster was right here and he was right here and he shot him right here. And, I mean, the whole back of his head was on the Dumpster [pause in tape] Magic Marker before the police got here and where *his brains* were went up like this and outlined it and after the police washed it down, they chalked the body after they washed all the blood down. And after they washed the blood off the Dumpster, they seen this mark and it was like someone who done this has, like, no sense. No one told on Ricardo because Ricardo was real crazy.

Just recently, there were four children caught in a terrible fire while their mothers were away from the building. I knew it was over a drug deal gone bad before the police ever arrived to question people. That is the way it is in the projects. Everybody knows everybody else's business. You know who's into drugs and where to buy them if you want them. You know all of the gangs and who belongs and which gangs get along and those that don't.

RK: And he blew up a house? And why did this guy do this?

IW: Because they said Karen (one of the mothers) took his dope. Karen did not take it. Andrew took it. And Andrew was selling it and he, Andrew, hid it under a rock. And she said that she did not have it, that she was walking to the store. And she left "Big Man" with the kids and they said the next thing they know they was all asleep and nobody heard him come in the house, but he came in the house and put the couch, chair, and loveseat together. Went in David's bedroom, it was her little brother, and took his clothes out of his drawer and dumped them in there. Went in there and went in her kitchen and got some bleach and he put her TV, stereo, she had four TVs in her house. He put them all around the couch and loveseat and put the stereo right in the middle. He had some gas with him. He put gasoline all around and bleach all the way around it. Then, as he was walking out the door, he flipped a cigarette in there. All that was so hot and it impacted at one time, and that is what exploded. All of them kids would have been dead if it had not been for "Big Man" dropping them kids out that window.

RK: So you live close to where that happened?

IW: No, that happened on the other side of town. But I know people who did it.

RK: So you are telling me that this is what life has been like?

IW: Yeah.

RK: For you?

IW: All my life I have been around violence!

If you live in the projects, the rules are different from those on the outside. I have been lucky enough to have had a few teachers who lived in the projects. They understand. When I attended Kingston, school went pretty well for me. The reason was that we were all poor and there was a pretty even mix of black and white. The same groups that had come to an understanding in the neighborhood carried that same understanding into school. We respected each other and got along with each other.

Then, school officials closed Kingston down over integration issues. I was forced to go to Jefferson Middle School—the most racist, richest school in the entire system. I am labeled as black because my father is black, my mother is white.

During that year at Jefferson Middle, I attended only fifty-four days out of the entire year and they still passed me. The white, rich kids knew exactly what to say to get me to "see red." When I see red, I am physical and out of control. There is no time to think, I just fight!

My dad raised me to accept people for who they are as individuals, and not to see color. Well, at Jefferson Middle, I was called "nigger," "nigger-honkie," and "nigger-ghonkie." My mom was called "nigger-lover." The rich kids use to come and put their heavy gold chain necklaces in my face and tell me how much they cost, at the same time mentioning that my family was probably on welfare. I was expelled so many times, but they wouldn't transfer me to another school or let me out. They kept saying they would deal with the problems themselves. They didn't want anyone to know just how bad things were. Or else they didn't care. They threatened me with 24-hour (mental) treatment, which means lock-up in a mental ward with no visitation. They threatened me with juvenile detention, but they wouldn't let me out of Jefferson Middle.

It was so bad, I even had teachers there announce at the beginning of a school year, "You blacks, leave me alone and stay out of my face. I don't want any trouble from you, see, because I don't like you very much."

My mom was there for me through all of this.

IW: Well, my mom, she don't put up with it. She has to know where I go and that is why I ain't been out in the projects. I got to be in the house. I am not allowed to go outside, you know, without my sister. So she ain't been letting me in the projects lately.

RK: That is an effort to keep you out of gang wars?

IW: Yeah, but she know I am not going. . . . I might fight but I am on probation. I really can't—I suppose to come in the house at 7:00 anyway.

RK: Really? Is that what the rules are?

IW: Yeah.

RK: What are some of the other probation rules?

IW: No drinking, no fights, not miss school; we have to go to school every day, no feuding at home, if you get out of the way with your parents, then they call and tell your probation officer. They will lock you up. You have to be home at curfew. You have to report to your probation officer if you going to be out of town. You can't go out of town without your probation officer's permission. You have to call two weeks before you going. No parties, no clubs, can't be around violence, can't be around anyone drinking. If you get caught at the scene of a crime, get caught in a club, you get locked up for thirty days.

My mom, she understands racism and hate. When I would lose my temper in official meetings in front of school principals, she would try to get me to respect my elders.

I am fourteen years old. I am a gang member. I have tried both alcohol and drugs. I have tried selling. I have been picked up by the police. I have spent time in juvenile detention. I have been expelled from and cannot attend most schools in the Brook County School System. I have a probation officer assigned by the courts. I have experienced day treatment at a mental health center. I have experienced (severe) depression.

Finally, at the end of 1992, I was released from Jefferson Middle to attend CAL. (Now it was their idea to release me from Jefferson Middle). I have not had one incident at this school and the academic year is more than half over. I am getting good grades again. I am attending school every day unless I am really sick. I get along well with my teacher, my counselor, my aide, and my classmates. My therapist is now a counselor at this school. I am still under treatment for depression.

When I look back at my early school years, I wonder if some of that pattern doesn't affect my schooling now. During my first four years of school, I spent the first half of every year in the North (Ohio) and the last half of every year in the South (Tennessee). The reason that happened was because my mom and dad were divorced and my dad lived in Ohio. Every summer I went to live with my dad. When school started in the fall, I was never ready to give up my friends and return home. So mom would let me stay until Christmas, but she wanted me home for Christmas. Then, I would attend the remainder of the academic year in Tennessee.

This worked well for me because the grades are more advanced in the North. Third grade in the North is similar to fourth grade in the South. That meant that I worked hard the first half of each academic year and coasted through the last half. I'm really smart, especially in math. So I never had trouble in school until I met racism face to face. My first encounter in school was when my teacher accused me of poor speech. She told me I talked funny and put me in Resource. (Resource is a classroom where special help is offered to slower students.) There were two teachers who used to argue over whether I was "slow" or "smart." But I remember doing my older sisters' homework for them, wondering why they thought it was difficult.

I want to be a professional football player when I grow up. I figure if I play football to get myself through college, I will study architecture so that I can earn a living when I get out. Or maybe I could be a professional ice skater when I grow up. I'm a good skater!

NARRATIVE DISCUSSION

Iesha's key event was being born "racial," as she called it. Her father was black and a northerner. Her mother was white and a southerner. Iesha had been taught by her father very early on that the color of a person's skin did not make the person. She expected to be treated according to the values her father had given her.

She did quite well for five years, kindergarten through fourth grade, attending Ohio schools in the fall and Tennessee schools after Christmas each year. Her reasons for being able to do well were twofold: Northern schools were approximately one year ahead of southern schools, and she had always done her older sisters' homework for them. She found school to be easy.

She spoke of her early teachers with love in her voice, remembering each one by name. In first grade, she was held back. She said her classmates and teachers told her she talked funny. But she remembered not being able to understand what she called "country" talk of her southern teacher. She said it sounded to her like, "I wearing a bird mop," nonsensical combinations of words that meant nothing to her. Putting her in Resource when she had always been in accelerated classes was one visual overlay for Iesha of teacher unfairness. But the ultimate unfairness came from what Iesha called "racial," when the projects school was closed and she was forced to attend the white, west-end middle school, the school Iesha called the rich school.

Her reports of teacher harassment because of her race were full of visual description. She spoke in detail of an incident in which a school helper, probably a parent, caused her and her best friend to be separated into different classes. Iesha believed this happened because her friend was white.

Another highly descriptive episode was one in which Iesha hit a teacher over the head with a lunch tray for separating her from the same white friend while they were in the cafeteria. She was told to sit next to a boy with body odor. The anger that was triggered by this incident was similar to other episodes interpreted by Iesha as issues stemming from racism.

Iesha also described having to wear her brother's coat in school because her teacher said she was dressed inappropriately. Iesha said that the incident stemmed from a white boy complimenting her on her outfit that day.

All of the violence, suicides, killings, and murders were described by Iesha in great detail. She could recall word for word the telephone conversation she had had with her boyfriend just before he shot himself in the head. She blamed herself for his death, as he had called, wanting to come and pick her up early for a party. While waiting, he had played Russian roulette with a partially loaded gun. She has been in treatment for severe depression because of all of the violence she has experienced in the last year.

School authorities said that she was unruly and had a bad attitude. She reported, however, that they would suspend her without listening to her side of any story. The principal, in front of Iesha's mother, accused Iesha of being prejudiced. The mother asked him how he thought Iesha could be prejudiced with a mother as white as she was!

Being black was not the only key event for Iesha. Being from the projects and being from a family on welfare were tied together almost as the same issue. Her defense of the value systems of families living in the projects as well as her description of rich Preps at Jefferson Middle were evidence of her understanding of the different treatment of the "haves" and the "have-nots." She underlined the connection between this understanding and the social backgrounds of her teachers when she contrasted the teacher who had lived in the projects with the teacher who could only say she understood what the projects were like. The latter teacher had a physician father and a lawyer husband.

Being black, living in the projects, and coming from a family on welfare were visual overlays that, to Iesha, justified violent and unruly behavior. She simply would not tolerate racist or antiwelfare remarks without a fight. Suspending her from school or threatening her with 24-hour treatment meant nothing to her since she felt justified in striking out over hostile comments.

In more than six months of nearly perfect attendance at CAL, she had not had one incident of unruly or violent behavior. In fact, the staff perceived that Iesha had leadership skills in the classroom.

While Iesha attended a neighborhood school close to the projects, she was not considered a troublemaker. When her neighborhood school was closed, she was forced to attend Jefferson Middle, which she considered to be the rich kids' school. Her behavior was rebellious, unruly, and uncontrollable; and she was expelled many more days than she attended school. After she was recommended to the Center for Alternative Learning, she once again became the model student. Her case resembles those of both Pam and D. J.—when the social setting changes, the student does not understand the rules in place that dictate appropriate behavior.

In addition to experiencing a change in social context, Iesha also wore a "label." Proponents of labeling theory state that the continuous interaction between the individual's behavior and the responses of others dictates how a person feels about himself or herself; one's identity and self-concept are affected by the reactions of others (Schur, 1971). As long as Iesha was accepted as an insider in her neighborhood school, she was not forced to respond in a rebellious way. Once Iesha was perceived or labeled by others as a misfit, her behavior changed dramatically. It appeared that Iesha's positive image of self demanded that she use violent behavior in an effort to defend black culture against racial slurs by whites. From the African American perspective, Iesha would be perceived as a leader for standing up to overt prejudice.

Iesha was labeled a black in a white, rich-kids' school. This stereotyping called "pictures in our minds" was explained by Walter Lippmann in 1922 and quoted from Schur (1971) as follows:

> We do not first see, then define, we define first and then see. . . .We are told about the world before we see it. We imagine most things before we experience them . . . and those preconceptions, unless education has made us acutely aware, govern deeply the whole process of perception. They mark out certain objects as familiar or strange, emphasizing the difference, so that the slightly familiar is seen as very familiar, and the somewhat strange as sharply alien. (p. 40)

Iesha's status as an outsider on multiple levels—an African American in a white-dominated school and a student from the projects among wealthy students—was the basis for the negative social interactions she experienced at Jefferson Middle School. Teachers overtly reinforced her outside status in the classroom. Iesha reported that one teacher even announced at the beginning of one class period, "You blacks don't get on my bad side 'cause I don't like niggers." This kind of stereotyping, based upon one personal physical characteristic of being either white or black, places the other on the defensive in social interaction.

Labeling theory also describes role engulfment, in the form of immersion in a deviant subculture, as a possible precondition for the individual's developing a strong deviant self-concept (Schur, 1971). Iesha's identity with gangs and gang culture in the projects appeared to place her in the adversarial position of defending the value system of African Americans and/or those of low socioeconomic meaning systems that contrasted with the white middle-class standards evidenced at Jefferson— standards that Iesha found offensive. Again, what came into play was the "looking-glass self." By reading body language and listening to what her peers said to her, Iesha quickly became aware that she was perceived as the outsider at Jefferson Middle, and the prejudice she experienced did not make her feel good about herself. The prejudice Iesha felt was real in its consequences for her.

RK: Can you tell me about your fifth-grade teacher and why you liked her?
IW: Well, she was, you know, trusting and honest and helped us out because she was once from the projects, too. And she understood what we was going through and all, the pressure we had on us in the projects. And she

used to keep our courage up high and tell us we could do it. You know, she did not think low of us, because she was from the projects.

Iesha then described gang membership. She spoke of gang fights that led to killings. She described unwritten rules about territory and drugs and beatings. She described violence as justified: "Because they beat up one of our boys. It was like twenty on one. They put him in the hospital for four weeks." "You can just get killed for saying 'Hi' in the wrong way."

Her meaning system had been learned as part of a gang culture that was foreign to me. Surely, just as Pam's Hoods had created a meaning-system change for Pam, Iesha's gang involvement had affected her meaning perspective about school. One readily apparent fact was that Iesha's looking-glass self was a person with integrity who would stand up and fight against racial remarks as if her life depended upon it.

In terms of anomie theory, Iesha was a "misfit" in the rich, white school she was forced to attend. She still had the cultural goal to do well in school and to attend college after high school graduation, but the institutional barriers represented by the school and its administrators were in place to keep her from accomplishing her educational goals. This placed her in Merton's "rebellion" category, similar to Pam Walker:

> When rebellion is confined to relatively small and relatively powerless elements in a community, it provides a potential for the formation of subgroups, alienated from the rest of the community but unified within themselves. This pattern is exemplified by alienated adolescents teaming up in gangs or becoming part of a youth movement with a distinctive subculture of its own. (1957, p. 140)

Once we hear the personal stories, a rationale for membership in gangs is more understandable. Each became alienated from the major group within the social context. In order to experience a sense of "belonging" somewhere, they turned to gang membership of one form or another.

CHAPTER 4

Delores Cook

Delores Cook was labeled a "troublemaker" by public school officials, and yet, was well liked and performed well at CAL. Her truancy behavior in regular school paralleled that of both Pam and Iesha: she sneaked out of her house at night to be with her chosen peer group for fun. After having a good time during the night with her friends, she was not willing to go to school the next day. She often pretended to be ill simply because she was tired.

Delores was seventeen years of age at the time the interviews took place. She was anticipating her eighteenth birthday in five and one-half months so she could "escape" the household in which she lived with her father, stepmother, brother, and cousin. Her mother, by failing to appear in court during the divorce process, had shown her lack of interest for custody of the children. When I asked why her cousin was a member of the household, she did not wish to talk about the subject except to indicate that everyone in the family knew that her father and her aunt "had something going." Her cousin was female, a year different in age from Delores. The cousin had already had an abortion, which made Delores very angry. She dismissed it as not being her issue.

Delores was an attractive, white female with short, blond hair and a very pretty smile. She was of medium height and build. She was ready to share almost any information about herself but was concerned about protecting the identity of others. Her refusal to reveal the identity of others was likely an attempt to protect herself from some "friends" who were capable of seriously harming her. She never spoke of a "best friend" other than the black males she was dating.

STUDENT NARRATIVE

I Never Wanted to Hurt My Daddy

DC: Yeah, 'cause my dad is, like, everything to me, 'cause he has always been there for me, always. You know how girls when they first have their first [pause] things, their mother is always there to help them through it and everything.

RK: So what happens when you go home after school?

DC: I just . . . if my dad is home, I just stay with my dad. If my dad is not home [her father drives a truck and is away for days at a time], I try to find someplace else to go. Over at my friends or something. When my dad is there, I want to stay there with my dad.

And then I ended up in the hospital emergency room with a blood alcohol level of 0.17. I had been beaten badly. The gold herringbone necklace that my daddy had given me had been stolen during the beating. I was caught! I had been sneaking out at night to be with my friends. We would stay up and party and talk. At first, I snuck out only when my dad was away driving a truck; later, I simply made sure that I got home before 6 a.m. But now he knew what I had been up to!

RK: So how did you begin drinking? Was that through school groups?

DC: My black friends. I got to where I was sneaking out of the house and going over to a person's house, this guy's house, and we would stay up and party and talk.

RK: This was at night you sneaked out?

DC: Yeah. Well, really, like, two o'clock in the morning. Then I would come back at six in the morning and I would not have no sleep for two or three days, just as long as my dad was gone. So one day I got, you know, I can't handle this, I have got to go somewhere and sleep. So I went over to a friend's house 'cause I couldn't just keep "laying out" [skipping school] and staying at home because that was what I was doing. The days I had ISS [in-school suspension], I went to school. I had two days of ISS. Then two days that I didn't have ISS, I stayed home. I complained that I was sick when I really wasn't. I was just . . . I really did not feel sick, I was just sleepy, you know, I was real sleepy.

I guess maybe it all started when I was in the eighth grade. A whole bunch of us used to smoke pot out in the back field, right at school. I remember one time my papaw (grandfather) was visiting: I snuck some of his beer out of the house and shared it with my friends at school. That same year, I began sneaking beer into the house so I could drink one before I went to school in the morning. Besides liking the taste, I used it to kind of relax me.

My dad didn't drink, but he kept Jack Daniels in the house for medicine. I liked the taste so much that I would pretend to be getting a cold so dad would tell me to get a sip to soothe my throat. I was, like, "Man, that is some good stuff."

I started sneaking Jack Daniels and drinking pure grain alcohol. I would go to my friend's house just up the road, and we would get drunk and smoke joints. One time I took some pills along with the other, and I didn't even know what they were! That was in the eighth grade.

> DC: I don't know, I just loved the taste of it. And then I just started drinking it. It was like some people have Coke in the morning—I wanted a beer. I was, like, I need that, you know, 'cause I would have beer snuck in my house. I would have people buy them for me and I would sneak them in my house. That is what I would drink in the morning before I went to school.

For a long time in the eighth grade, I smoked a joint every morning and every lunch period along with my friends, just to get relaxed. One time, we all got caught taking pills before a history test. The pills were supposed to help us pass the test, according to the guy passing them out. After we got caught, the story was that the school was going to run drug tests on all of us, so there I was in the girls' room trying to puke up those pills. The tests were never run, but all parents of involved students were called to school. Even though my cousin and I were both in the girls' room at the same time, I was the one accused of supplying everyone. But it wasn't me, it was one of the guys. I'm not sure anyone ever believed me though, especially my dad. When we got home from school that day, I wanted to help cook in the kitchen. My daddy really hurt my feelings, because he said, "No, you might put some drugs in our food or something."

In eighth grade, one of my teachers got wise. We were all sleeping in his class one day, heads down on our desks. See, smoking pot and drinking beer both enhance the effects of your mood of the day. If you are hyper, it makes you more hyper; if you are relaxed, it relaxes you more. We had all been out in the back field for lunch smoking and drinking. He would slap a ruler against a table trying to wake us up and get our attention. Then we got the lecture about using drugs. But the strange thing is, he never told anyone about the incident. He never did anything about it.

That was eighth grade. In ninth grade, I was too paranoid to get into much trouble. I had entered a new school. I took my bad reputation with me, so I was extra careful in ninth grade.

In tenth grade, I started hanging out with black guys. My dad is really prejudiced so I had to sneak around and be dishonest with my parents. I dated two black guys who were cousins. I went with one, Roshawn, for about six or seven months. Then I met Anthony at a restaurant one night. I have never seen anyone so handsome in my whole life. He still gives me butterflies when I see him. I never thought I would date blacks because of the way my daddy feels, but Anthony is so gorgeous! And he makes me feel so good about myself. You know, he puts me way up on a pedestal. I can't believe he dates me.

> RK: Has your dad ever asked you why you like to date black guys?
> DC: He doesn't approve of it. He gets mad every time he finds out. So I just don't want him to know. And I want to see . . . like, a black guy I am going out with, I am talking to one right now, I have to sneak around, you know. I hate doing that. Because I am being dishonest with my parents. It is, like, the only way I can [see him]. It seems to me that black guys treat me better. They put me on a pedestal. And a white guy doesn't. It's like he don't see me for what I am.

But Anthony is the one who had me beat up. He got so jealous, especially if I talked to his cousin, the one I used to date. He was the reason I don't trust blacks anymore. This was how the beating happened so that I ended up in the emergency room.

I had been sneaking out with this guy, Anthony, and one night he called me. He wanted to know if I had been talking to his cousin. He got real upset with me. He said, "I am coming to get you." I was excited because I was going to get out of the house. Usually when they came for me, I would get in the front seat, but he said, "You are sitting in the back seat this time because you are being punished." At this point, I thought it was a big joke. We got to Sammy's house and both cousins were there. I was leaning up against Anthony's body when Roshawn walked in. It made me feel uncomfortable with both of them in the same room, so I got up and went to the bathroom. After Roshawn left about 5 a.m., I leaned back against Anthony again. He said, "No, no, just get off me now. If you didn't want to lay on me while Roshawn was here, then get off me now." It was like a major temper tantrum. We got into a "yes" and "no" battle and I punched him really hard in the stomach. He smacked me very hard on top of my head and held me in a head lock. I fell asleep in the choke hold; I was real tired. I had only one or two beers. That night I went home.

The next day I went to Sammy's house to see Anthony. Anthony said, "What the hell are you doing here?" I said, "I came back to be with you." We laid on the couch together and slept through the entire day. After we got up, Anthony was getting ready to go to the mall when his ex-girlfriend arrived. She had had a baby by Anthony. I had never talked to her before so I thought I wouldn't like her. We hit it off real well. She and I talked everything out, but I could tell that Anthony was still really mad. He told Sammy to take me home, but I wouldn't go with him. I decided to wait for Anthony. Sammy said, "Man, come on, you know he ain't coming back for you. He didn't want to see you anyway." It was after 3:30 p.m., and I was supposed to be back at school because my parents pick me up every day at that time. So I called my mamaw's (grandmother's) house. My cousin, the one who lives with us, told me that my dad had kicked me out of the house.

Well, that was it! I just drank trying to drown my problems. I wanted to feel better and forget the mess I was in. I drank a quart of Bud and a quart of Red Bull. I got blasted. Sammy got scared and called my friend Danny to take me home. I was so drunk! I said, "Don't take me home. Take me back to Sammy's (house)." I was so drunk, I would have got out of the car while it was going rather than face my father. When we got back to Sammy's, I crawled up onto the front porch. I don't know how I got to the couch inside. I know my shoes were off and that I was about to pass out. About that time, this big black woman came in and started beating me up. She stole the gold necklace my daddy had given me. I was weak. I couldn't do nothing 'cause I was just so drunk. And next thing I know, I'm in the emergency room and my daddy was there. I never wanted to hurt my daddy.

To this day, I won't tolerate anyone smacking me around. From the time my daddy remarried (I was about six years old) until I was fourteen, my stepmother smacked me around when my daddy wasn't around. I was three or four when my parents divorced. My worst memory is of me clinging to my daddy's legs and the police trying to drag him to jail. My daddy and I lived together for about three years after the divorce. He and I got real close. The police came because my mother reported that he kept her from seeing me. That was a lie!

DC: And I remember my mother called the cops on my dad 'cause she said that he refused to let us [Delores and her brother] go with her—when he didn't. And he got put in jail and it killed me. I was holding on to my daddy's legs while they was telling him . . . I remember the exact thing. They knocked on the door, he come to the door, and I was standing behind him 'cause I always followed him and they told him to remove everything from his pockets—so he did. Then they said, "You are under arrest." I was holding on to him saying, "Daddy please don't leave, please don't leave me." But he had to go. It upset me really bad.

I remember how much I hated my stepmom after my dad remarried. She could never take the place of my mother.

> DC: I hated her. I was, like . . . no, you are trying to take the place of my mother and you are never going to do it. I just hated her for it. I did not think she loved my dad. I was like—you don't love him, you are trying to make our life miserable.
>
> She used to slap me around a lot. I mean I was tiny. He didn't know it until one night he was upstairs asleep and I said something about her mother. I said, "I am not going over there, that brat," talking about my uncle. Well, she slapped me in the face, and I was down there and she was smacking me around. And my dad came down there and he got mad.

Like kids at school, I would not take any crap off anyone at school, and I felt like that kind of brought it on me too. 'Cause, I was, like . . . you know . . . I always had anger or hatred built up in me. So when I got mad at somebody, I did not hold it in 'cause it was like a little bit too much. I would always end up getting in a fight. And then I carried that reputation to Madison (High School) with me.

Because my dad filed a petition with the juvenile authorities charging me with public drunkenness, I have to appear in court next week, I have to pay $60. I have to go to drug and alcohol school and pass it. If I don't pass, then I have to pay $25. I have to go for a month. Four days out of the month." I just got a job in order to pay my bills. I am training right now, but after that I will be working full time besides going to school. (Author note: Delores is not legally allowed to work forty hours per week, but she represents a way in which students begin a pattern of dropping out of school. With males, it is to earn money to buy a car.)

I need to make money so that I can move out when I turn eighteen in five and one-half months. I can't wait to move out.

> RK: Why do you feel so strongly about wanting to move out of the house where you live now?
> DC: 'Cause I hate it, I hate it so much.
> RK: And tell me what you hate about it.
> DC: I hate our rules and everything.

The only way out right now is to elope with Anthony or have a baby by him. I don't want to get pregnant by him, but if he asked me to marry him right now, I would do it in a minute. Just to get out of my house. I would run away with the guy who had me beat up—just to get out!

NARRATIVE DISCUSSION

For Delores, a key event in her life was the divorce of her mother and father when she was about four years old. The key event with the richest description was her memory of clinging to her daddy's legs as the police came to put him in jail when she was six years old. Another key event was that of being rejected by her mother. Her mother had acted out her lack of desire for custody of Delores and her brother by not appearing in court. This did not go unnoticed by Delores. This was rejection.

Tied to Delores's description of the divorce events was her description of living with her father before his second marriage. She described a time when she had her father's undivided attention—not unlike some of the descriptions by Pam Walker. Delores could not remember much about a dating process by her father nor about his marriage to her stepmother.

Another visual overlay was the "slapping around" she described in her story and a major desire on her part to escape from the household. Even though she knew Anthony might be a drug dealer (he always wore a beeper and drove a very fancy car), she denied this as a possible truth. She saw Anthony as her only way out. She admitted that she would elope with Anthony if she were given the opportunity, even though he had arranged for her beating (according to Delores).

She felt the key event for her lack of interest in school to be her friendships with black males; her dating of black males; and her smoking, drinking, and sneaking out at night as a result of her association with this group. It is obvious that Delores was looking for peer acceptance, just as others in the study had done. At the beginning of the interview sessions, she said she would never trust a black boyfriend again. By the end of our interviews, she was sneaking out at night to meet Anthony again. In fact, she was extremely anxious for a while, believing she might be pregnant by Anthony. Like Pam Walker, Delores admitted that she sneaked out at night and skipped school in the day. Delores also became ill from being so exhausted from her night life. Some of Delores's extreme behavior may have been an effort on her part to get her father's attention and to hurt him.

The major drinking episode that put her in the emergency room with a blood alcohol level of 0.17 was because her cousin had informed her on the telephone that her daddy had kicked her out of the house. She said that if her daddy was going to be mad at her, then she simply did not care what happened to her. The reasons she gave for being so in love with Anthony were that he was gorgeous, he put her on a pedestal, and he acted out his jealousy of her in front of others. To Delores, this meant that he cared about her. She also felt certain that Anthony was the one who had arranged for her beating. He had promised to "make it up to her, to take care of her, and to buy her a new gold chain."

Delores's low impulse control in order to meet her short-term needs without thinking of any long-term consequences is typical of pushouts. They have a fatalistic attitude about life so that there is no plan for the future; and, therefore, no sense of consequences over poor choices that they make now. She had been labeled a troublemaker. She and her cousin, who live together as sisters, are treated very differently by the school principal. Now Delores is at further risk because she is trying to work full time while going to school.

The divorce of Delores's parents was a key event in her life history, for several reasons. For a period of time after the divorce and before his remarriage, she and her father were very close; she remembered this time as a good time in her life. Delores perceived her mother's failure to ask for custody of her as a personal rejection that created a deep wound. Finally, her father's remarriage introduced a stepmother into the household who mistreated (slapped her around) her. In Merton's (1957) terms, Delores had lost her "place" of belonging within the home as well as losing her own sense of power. This is similar to D. J.'s being rejected by his family as well as Pam's perception of rejection by her father.

Delores described the racial prejudice of both her father and her biological mother. It appeared that Delores's seeking a place for herself on a pedestal within a black-male group was not only motivated sexually but was also an act to gain power or control over her own life (Glasser, 1986). Delores described a need to feel placed "on a pedestal" and that only black boyfriends made her feel this way.

Delores was labeled by school authorities as a troublemaker and was treated in a similar way to that described by D. J. When Delores and her cousin were caught in the girls' room, the cousin was sent back to the classroom, but Delores was given in-school suspension. When there was a classroom problem of someone's handing out drugs before a history test, Delores was held responsible for the incident even though she named the young man who had been the supplier. These are examples of how students are stereotyped by school officials, and how this can affect a student's meaning perspective toward school (Schur, 1971). Both Iesha and Delores requested placement outside of their respective schools because of having a "reputation," and yet both were held within the system for undue lengths of time. Both served many days of suspension, which only contributed to their getting further behind in academic work.

For Delores, the strong goal was no longer academic achievement but escape from the household in which she lived. She did expect to graduate from high school as her means of getting a job to support an independent life. She did not dismiss running away with Anthony as one possible avenue of escape.

She blamed her association with the black peer group as the beginning of her problems in school. Her pattern of sneaking out of the house when her father was on the road driving a truck was similar to that of Pam Walker. Pam, Iesha, and Delores each first joined a peer group that supported truancy and antischool and antiauthority behaviors and secondarily got into academic trouble at school. Each pretended illness to avoid school attendance and to associate with an outside group.

In the first four chapters, I have discussed key events and visual overlays described by each of the four case studies. Key events in students' lives that kept them from functioning well in school were linked to family life or peer groups and were rarely linked to school-related reasons. Three of the four students talked about not being able to concentrate in school when they had concerns from the outside. Problems involving parents or a student's sex life were especially disruptive to the learning process.

These key events and visual overlays affected the way in which each of these students chose to interact with peers, with teachers, and with school officials. It was easy for them to justify their position from the meaning perspective that each held. School suspension appeared to have little impact on these students. As D. J. said, being suspended only meant that the pushout needed to be "more slick" the next time around in order to outsmart the system.

Now that I have presented four case studies in detail, I will pool all of the data gathered from the interviews, present the themes in Chapter 5 that emerged, and discuss in Chapter 6 the findings. For those of you who are interested in this study from a research perspective, the doctoral dissertation by Rosa Lea Kennedy entitled *A Study of Four Student Pushouts from the Perspective of Four Sociological Theories* (University of Tennessee, Knoxville, 1993) is available from University of Michigan, Ann Arbor. The middle chapters present basic teaching concepts and strategies that every teacher should know when dealing with this type of student. The final chapters present the new paradigm for implementing a school for healing and alternative learning.

CHAPTER 5

Emerging Themes

Each of the four students spoke of a time when he or she enjoyed school and liked the teachers. Two of the four said, "I just loved my teacher." Iesha had had many teachers that she "just loved" and could call each by name. D. J. spoke of school on the beach with great pleasure. These were his early years when he wrote stories and "messed with the girls" in the second grade. This was his California experience.

The key events that triggered the beginning of school hatred and the student's alienation with school were:

1. a major move,
2. illegal drug use and violence in the home,
3. perceived racism issues, or
4. the divorce and subsequent remarriage of a parent.

These events triggered a change in meaning perspective about school. Table 5.1 is a comparison of student life events that affected their school interactions.

One can see that commonalities were found across the studies, but not always in the same combinations. Each of the four participants had experienced being held back a grade for differing reasons. This supports the literature on "dropouts," which finds that being held back a year in the early grades is a "predictor variable" to look for with dropouts.

Drug use usually gets students into deep trouble educationally, but this study goes further to say that drugs are not always introduced through school. That D. J.'s parents introduced him to the habit at a very young age was not something that I had encountered in the literature about dropouts. Iesha's use of drugs appeared to be short term and experimental, directly connected to her membership in the street gang of the projects. She had actually sold drugs for a very short period just to see what it was like.

Table 5.1
A Comparison of Student Life Events That Affected Their School Interaction

	Student #1	#2	#3	#4
Grade Failure	x	x	x	x
Drug Use		x	x	x
Sneaking Out	x			x
Feigned Sickness	x	x	x	x
Major Moves	x	x	x	
Violence		x	x	x
Unfair Teachers	x	x	x	x
Parental Divorce		x	x	x

Sneaking out and feigned sickness are more prevalent in our society than most parents believe to be true. This common behavior may help justify the curfew that teenagers object to so much.

Major moves across the country are extremely disruptive to students. School rules change dramatically from one system to another and even between schools in the same district. If we as educators would acknowledge the trauma that a student making a major move from one part of the country to another experiences, some solutions could be adopted to help students make the transition. Feeling like an outsider to a social group, such as a school classroom, can nudge teenagers to join an antischool group.

Experiencing violence, whether at home, within the neighborhood, or at school, is detrimental to a positive educational process. During class time, the student's focus is on remembered or current violence rather than on the learning process.

Teacher unfairness is linked with the ideas that teachers assume that all students want to continue with a college education, and especially with the feeling that teachers identify more strongly with middle to upper middle-class socioeconomic groups. Most people who pursue a teaching career hold middle-class values that include a belief in education as a means of getting ahead. Students living in poverty may not have parental support for this goal. The students in the study perceived that teachers and principals enforced rules differently for different students. Jocks and cheerleaders got preferential treatment at school. Cheerleaders and athletes generally come from middle and upper socioeconomic families.

Of the issues listed in Table 5.1, only that of teacher favoritism appears to be a school issue. Kronick and Hargis (1990) discussed the issue of teacher favoritism. They found that teachers favored those students who were raised in family situations closest to their own—especially socioeconomic status. However, the themes that emerged from the pooled data of this study were drug and alcohol prevalence among students, perceived teacher favoritism, and gang involvement and peer-group influence.

NARRATIVE DISCUSSION

Substance abuse generally began within the family context and later became an issue in school. D. J. was given marijuana through a straw up his nose as a newborn infant and later smoked pot with his mom as afternoon entertainment while watching cartoons. Delores was introduced to pot by a friend's father when she was in the eighth grade. To hear that students take unknown pills along with alcohol should give us a clue about just how naive teenagers are about the dangers of drugs. Both Delores and Iesha were given small amounts of liquor within the home. Delores was given Jack Daniels as medication for colds. She acquired a taste for it that developed into what she termed addiction. By the time Delores was in the eighth grade, she was combining alcohol and smoking pot in order to achieve a greater high. This took place on the school grounds with a group of friends when she was approximately thirteen years old. Iesha was given sips of beer that her biological mother drank as "medication for kidney problems." At the time, Iesha was only three years old. Iesha later developed a drinking problem that, with the encouragement of her boyfriend, she was able to control.

Quotations from the interviews that support the data above include the following:

DC: Yeah, well in middle school, too, in the eighth grade, we would smoke a joint every morning before we went to school. Like, maybe, the last semester I smoked a joint every morning before we went to school. We would smoke a joint every lunchtime every day out in the field. *And nobody ever knew* [emphasis added].

RK: You had to be in the in-group [to smoke]?

DC: No, whoever wanted it [could have it]. We got to where one time, my papaw was in visiting and he was always drunk, so I stole some of his beers and we . . . I mean I had a big cup of beer and I would take it to school and mixed it with some Jack Daniels, and we all drunk that with our pot.

RK: So if you drank beer or Jack Daniels with pot what happens?

DC: I don't know, it kind of gives you more high.

RK: Makes you more high than if you do either one by itself?

DC: 'Cause you kind of take on the actions . . . . If you get high and you're in a happy mood, you get real hyper. If you are in a sad mood, you get real depressed.

RK: Eighth grade, so a lot of this started in the eighth grade?

DC: Yeah, one night, we . . . in the ninth grade, we would go to YOKE [a young people's church group]. We would go out, get drunk, smoke some pot. One time I remember us climbing on top of Ridgecrest, on top of the roof, drinking with this guy. We were drinking some vodka or something. I would come in drunk every Tuesday night. My parents, my mom would never know. My dad wasn't there, but my mom would never know.

Iesha was only fourteen at the time of the interview. She admitted having had an alcohol problem at one time.

IW: My dad knew nothing about it [her drinking habit] till it was too late. I was about nine years old when my dad finally found out I had been drinking. My dad, you know, he couldn't stop it, so it, you know, I mean you, he could not contribute to it, but it was my choice. My dad always gave his kids choice. And he lets us learn. My daddy is not the type person who is going to say, "Well, don't do it." He is going to let you learn from your mistakes.

RK: Are you the one who decided to quit? With his help?

IW: Well, it wasn't like that. I drunk and drunk and I and a cousin who just loved it. She loved to see me drunk.

RK: So what were you drinking then, beer or stronger?

IW: I used to drink nothing but gin and everyone else would drink it with a chaser, but I am the youngest one out of the bunch, but I would not use a chaser. And everyone used to be curious why I am like that. And she never contributed to that, but my mom's stepbrother does for a while, but still—

RK: This was the cousin you say that liked to see you drunk?

IW: Then my sisters would drink at a party or something. I would say, "Hey, I am going over in the corner. I am going to drink me some too." But then finally, you know, I started thinking, you know, I had John, my boyfriend who shot himself, he would make you think. He would get down to it and make you think about things. Well, he wasn't the type to drink. He got down to the nitty-gritty. I mean, he said, "Do you know what you are doing to yourself?" And he made me go home one night and really think. I don't need it. I got a whole life in front of me. And you know, he was this kind of person that you really talk to and he would tell you straight up and say, "You know, I [you] don't really need this."

RK: Is alcohol more of a problem in the projects than drugs?

IW: Among young teens, alcohol is a big problem. But also marijuana is a very big problem.

RK: Is it easy to get marijuana in the projects?

IW: Yeah, you, hey!

RK: You have to have money, don't you?

IW: Yeah. Unless you got the right friend. And I was pressured a couple of times to smoke marijuana and sometimes I did, but, you know, I know now, hey, I will never try the stuff again, 'cause I turn blue in the face. 'Cause something about it, they said I inhaled it wrong or something, and I just started choking and I couldn't breathe.

Iesha also described how a girl at Jefferson Middle School had tried to set her up by asking her to bring marijuana to school. But Iesha claimed that she didn't "do that stuff no more."

D. J. and his friend John, who had recently graduated from high school, spoke about the prevalence of drugs within the family and within the community.

RK: Was it in Tennessee or New Orleans when you and your mom smoked pot together?

DJ: Tennessee, but I remember before that in New Orleans, me and my cousins used to smoke it.

RK: So how did you have this readily available? Does everybody in your family smoke? Your dad must not.

DJ: Everybody I know does. Is that not true, John? Almost everybody does.

RK: So it is the Tennessee thing to do; is it easily accessible here?

John: It is easily accessible anywhere. There is so many do it. Just as many people do it, if not more, than don't. Lot won't admit it, but—

DJ: Yeah, I don't think of it as anything wrong though. Me and M. and all of us would smoke pot sometimes in the morning over at Glacial Springs and then walk over to auto mechanics. It was fun!

DJ: [Talking about smoking at school] I think they [the teachers] kind of understand that when you smoke [regular cigarettes] and you don't have a cigarette for a long time, you get nervous and that is going to mess with you. I think you should be allowed to smoke.

Of the four participants in the study, not one was introduced to drug or alcohol use at school. It appeared that substance abuse began within the family or community and infiltrated the school system as a problem from society at large. School officials did not appear to be very well informed about substance-abuse behavior. Delores described in detail the time when her history class was asleep in their seats from the noonday smoke and drink session on the school grounds. The teacher rapped a ruler sharply on the desk in an effort to awaken them. He then lectured them on substance abuse but never reported them, nor did he follow through in any way. It appeared that both parents and school officials were either naive about the symptoms or chose to ignore the problem until the behavior was well engrained.

TEACHER FAVORITISM

A second major theme that emerged during this study was that of teacher favoritism. The Preps and cheerleading competitions were also mentioned independently by each of the three females as an example of teacher favoritism in the schools. From the student perspective, the three categories of teacher favoritism, cheerleading competition, and the Preps were presented as one issue.

The Preps were described as rich, white, all-A students who strove to be perfect in dress as well as in classroom work. Teachers could justify their position by saying that students who strive to do their best on assignments are rewarded by special privileges. The students with special privileges viewed this issue differently. The students who are teacher favorites never question the favoritism; they simply enjoy their privilege. Pam was not one of the favorites because she was a northerner in a southern school. In the North she had enjoyed being one of the privileged. D. J. said that he was stereotyped because of his long hair. He also had the reputation of being a marijuana user as well as coming from a home without running water. D. J. also did not participate in school activities, especially sports. He would have had transportation problems for any after-school activity.

D. J. spoke of teacher favoritism only in regard to Jocks. Jocks did not have to attend math class; received passing grades on their exams; and, therefore, received passing grades for the course. D. J. assumed that the Jocks already had the math skills necessary to pass the course rather than perceiving this to be teacher favoritism. D. J. did state at the conclusion of his description that the math teacher was also a coach.

Iesha's description of Preps and "Teacher Preps" (her term) and the interrelationship of the two can be found as quoted material at the end of this discussion. She also described a classroom episode in which all of the favorites gathered around the teacher and Iesha, as she entered the classroom, was directed to sit in the far back corner. Because she refused to do this, she was expelled from school. She perceived this incident to be teacher favoritism. Since Iesha had been labeled "unruly" by this school system, the teacher could probably justify his or her position as a decision to separate Iesha from the group in order to maintain classroom order.

Delores described teachers using school rules as a power play against the least-favored student. For example, she was physically ill in the girls room one day. Her cousin, who lived within the same family as Delores, was with Delores as a caregiver. Both came out of the restroom together.

Her cousin was sent back to her room with no consequences. Delores was told by the principal that she was not sick, that she was in the hall without a hall pass, and that she needed to go to the office and wait for the arrival of her parent, who would be called. Delores was given in-school suspension because of this episode. She refused to serve her time, stating that the principal was lying. Her father finally believed Delores's account over the principal's account because of the intensity of Delores's reaction. Delores's father knew that she would take her punishment if she was in the wrong. He also knew that she became extremely agitated when someone was lying to her. In this conflict, Delores, in front of her father, had told the principal to "kiss her ass." This was out of character for Delores, who was expected by her father to respect school officials.

Iesha also described situations in which she felt wrongly accused of instigating school fights. She would be expelled without being given an opportunity to tell her side of the story. This is dehumanizing action on the part of school officials and is documented in the literature (Woods, 1979). When students are not given the opportunity to tell their side of a story, but are simply expelled, this action makes students feel extremely vulnerable.

The anger represented in the student interviews concerning Preps is understandable, since Preps and teacher favoritism were linked together in the minds of the students' meaning perspective in this study. Following is Iesha's description of Preps and "Teacher Preps":

IW: OK, this girl last year named Buffy Mills. I mean, her clothes had to be perfect, her hair had to be perfectly curled, her fingernails had to be perfect. Her makeup had to be perfect and everything about her just had to be perfect. No one could beat her, she thought she was everything because she was a cheerleader. And she used to walk around flashing her money and talking about how much money she had. If she seen a person who didn't look as wealthy as her, she would talk about them. She would say, "You look like you ain't got no money." And she would say, "Are you on welfare?" And stuff like that. And she was just the biggest snob there, and she used to just walk around looking primpy—go in the mirror after every period—go in the bathroom and primp in the mirror. She said, "Oh, does my hair look all right?" It used to get on everybody's nerves and I . . . some of the white kids wanted to beat her up because she thought she was Miss Perfect. I mean, if she got a B on her work she would cry. That is how perfect she had to be. And everything she did had to be perfect.

We had to write a report about a state; she brought in more like a book. It had to be perfectly typed and, I mean, she could not miss a word. Everything was spelled correct. She said "I even used my encyclopedia." I mean, she used to come to school and say, "Do you see this charm bracelet, it cost $12.99 and each charm I add to it cost $20 apiece." And she had already about fifty charms and every day, she would come in with a new charm on it. "Do you see my charm?" I just wanted to rip her little charm bracelet off and throw it up against the window. 'Cause she loved her little charm bracelet.

And, I mean, her hair bows, "My hair bows cost this and that." She had braces: She would actually break them, she would sit and pick on them until she broke them. Then say, "Oh, that is another $500 my dad has to pay." And she used to say, "My braces cost $5,000." 'Cause she had the clear kind and I mean, everything, her hair, and she was talking about she used to wear glasses, then she got contacts. She has green contacts and swore up and down her eyes were green. And they were like a brown blue. I mean, she was just . . . Miss Perfect. Nothing could go wrong and then, one day, she fell, and that was the biggest thing. We hated her. She fell and everybody started laughing and she got up crying and she said, "Well, I am going to tell my dad and he's going to get a lawyer and he is going to sue all of you for laughing at me." And she just, ohhhhhhhhhh, we just hated her.

IW: The cheerleading teacher. She taught science, but she was also with the cheerleaders. She . . . her and Buffy . . . I thought they were mommy and daughter, first time I met them. 'Cause Miss Primps . . .she picked Buffy, not for her talent in cheerleading, because she . . . but because Buffy was so much like her. Buffy couldn't even jump. But she picked her. Buffy was so much like her.

RK: And she said what?

IW: Yeah, she—there was one girl named Taja on the cheerleading squad . . . who was real sweet and Taja asked her [the cheerleading teacher] why she picked Buffy over this girl named Carol? Carol has real good jumps, but she is not the person, she is not real outgoing and she keeps to herself, but, you know, she is fun to be with, and stuff, if you get to know her. And she didn't pick her because she didn't talk as much and she picked Buffy because she was more like her. And, I mean, the teacher use to stand around ever five minutes putting on her lipstick, or fixing her hair, up there primping, and I think she had a crush on another science teacher. She would just start blushing and think that she was pretty, and her clothes! When she taught the girls how to cheer, she taught the girls in church shoes and in a skirt, and a nice neat blouse. I mean, she would not put on a jogging suit, or pair of shorts.

RK: Were there competitions for cheerleading? Did you think they were fair?

IW: Sometimes I thought they was fair, and then again, I didn't 'cause a black girl named Letha tried out and Letha was real good. She could do the split, the high toe touch. I mean, she was a real good cheerleader. And the only thing . . . the reason she didn't get it is because they wanted the money right up front and her dad said that he would pay it when he got his paycheck.

RK: I don't understand "money up front." You mean you had to pay to compete or what?

IW: You had to pay. Like if she would have made it, you would have to had paid the money the day they said you made it. And her dad said he didn't get his pay check for another two weeks, so he would pay it then. Well, she said, "Well, I can't wait on that." And I didn't think that was fair because the money would get paid. She was a good cheerleader. I think they should have went ahead and let her did it, but . . . one girl, Bridget, she paid hers in three installments. But they would not let [Letha].

RK: What was this money for?

IW: For your uniforms, shoes, socks, your earrings, socks, stockings, jackets.

RK: Things that look alike?

IW: Yeah, I mean, they had book bags, jogging suits, socks, stockings, tennis shoes, hair bows, sweatbands, I mean everything.

RK: So what kind of money are we talking about?

IW: Five hundred and fifty dollars. And that was just for middle school. Five hundred and fifty dollars. I said, "Mom, I am going to try out for the cheerleading squad." She said, "Do you really want to do this?" I said, "Yes." And then she was like for sure you want to do this, if you make it you are not going to drop out. I said, "Forget it, I don't want to do it." Because it is not but a one-year thing and they change uniforms every year. So if you make it the next year, you have to buy a whole new uniform, new tennis shoes, everything . . . they get everything new each year. They will not have the same uniform for two years. That is just a rich, preppy school.

PEER-GROUP INFLUENCE

A third major theme that emerged from the interviews was peer-group influence. Pam, in her description of peers, introduced only Preps, Jocks, and Hoods as choices for group membership at her school. In contrast, Iesha described many different gangs as well as a definition of turf or territory. The difference in description appeared to be the cultural context: West Brookton is comprised of families from upper SES groups while the projects are comprised of families from lower SES groups.

The projects, according to Iesha, could only be understood by someone who had lived there. She had witnessed or known of twenty-five stabbings and killings, including deaths by suicide, in her lifetime. Several of these were gang related. She described turf and territory as issues she had grown up with and understood. In contrast, Pam had to learn from the Hoods how to skip school for action and excitement in her life.

Farrell (1990) described the influences of peer culture for at-risk students as follows:

> What we as adults see as adaptive behaviors do not always seem to have a payoff to young people. Our notions of adaptive behaviors, e.g., staying in and doing your home work rather than hanging out with friends, seem to them to be

maladaptive. Your peers give you more reinforcement. . . . From peers you learn techniques of self-expression and social interaction. Avoiding peers (from the student perspective) is maladaptive. If there is no future in hanging out, well, there's not much future in school either. And hanging out is much more enjoyable.

If the values you construct with peers are disdained by parents, teachers, and the greater society, you might come to disdain the competing values, if only as a defense. (p. 25)

Peer-group influence may be antischool, and behavior that supported the antischool meaning perspective was learned as social interaction within the group.

Iesha compared her neighborhood projects' school (which was closed down) to the West Brookton school to which she had been assigned. She noted that at Washington Heights everyone was poor, black and white alike. Since all of the students had grown up together, they understood each other. As a result, there were relatively few issues brought up at school that had not been dealt with in the neighborhood. The Washington Heights school practiced conflict resolution, which forced the two embattled factions to face each other and attempt to work through the issues at hand. This may have prevented physical fights.

In contrast to the Washington Heights school, the West Brookton school was represented as the rich, preppy school where a poor, black student whose family was on welfare found it difficult to succeed. Iesha provided detailed descriptions of a Prep flashing money around, announcing how much her braces cost, and asking Iesha if her family was on welfare. Many differences among the students appeared to be heightened when students from widely varied class backgrounds were thrown together at school with little preparation. Further, Iesha's perception was that there were no efforts in the wealthy school to introduce conflict resolution. One was expelled with no opportunity to defend one's position. As a result, Iesha was only more anxious to finish a fight when she returned to school because she had been suspended.

Two participants, Iesha and Delores, described wanting to leave their school situation by means of a student transfer. In both cases, school officials were unwilling to release them. The school authorities argued that students should have to work through their problems. From the student perspective, no effort was made to resolve issues and nothing changed. Both students described being forced into a position of sitting isolated in a classroom with head on desk, often sleeping through class in order to avoid further confrontation.

Violence in the wider social context is infiltrating the schools. In 1992, the Brook County School System located loaded guns and had bomb scares in the school buildings among children as young as fifth graders. D. J. walked away from school one day because he had been threatened by a bully. Iesha described how teachers were afraid to enter the hallways when students were changing from one class to another. Hate speech between students often triggered major physical confrontations. Iesha said that she would not attend a football game without "something on her." When I asked her to describe what she meant, she said she would not attend a football game without a knife for protection. It appears that gangs and violence and substance abuse are infiltrating our schools from the outside in.

Of the three major themes, drug and alcohol prevalence, teacher favoritism, and gangs or peer-group influence, it appeared that the only issue pinpointed by students as an issue internal to the school systems was that of teacher favoritism. Even teacher favoritism is linked to socioeconomic status and is, therefore, an "outside" issue. The issues, then, infiltrated the schools from the family or the community at large. This study gave a wider perspective to the pushout problem than simply that of a school at fault or a student at fault. To become aware of the student's wider social context as a continuum of ongoing events, often precipitated by family members or the family members of very young peers within a neighborhood, is to say that there were circumstances in place that were beyond the control of either the student or the school system. In the past, the fault had been directed at either student or school. School officials must care enough about the individual student to assess problems early on— whether they are personal problems, family problems, or learning difficulties. Prolonged truancy without immediate attention on the part of school officials sets up a series of events that promotes student failure and subsequent dropping out. The loss to the individual student and the loss to society is too great.

CHAPTER 6

Discussion

Four student narratives were presented from teenagers expelled from school—students no longer welcome in the public school classroom. Such students are first labeled "students at risk of dropping out of school" by school officials and researchers. They soon become "pushouts," students singled out and expelled so many times that remaining in school becomes a challenge to the student. Instead, the student often turns to a peer group for positive social interaction. Too often, these peer groups, or gangs, teach the new member the antischool, antiauthority meaning perspectives that support dropping out of school as a viable choice. In this chapter, I will compare my findings to similar studies conducted in other parts of the country.

In contrast to a medical model that blames failure at school to deficits within the child, an anthropological model looks for reasons that explain the behavior of students at risk.

> An anthropological perspective insists that every individual does his or her best to preserve self-esteem and (to) survive as an intact person. This struggle to preserve and survive often results in behavior that is perceived as deviant, destructive, and dysfunctional by observers who are operating out of different contexts. (Trueba, Spindler, & Spindler, 1989, p. 1)

Clearly some students drop out of school in an attempt to find a social structure that validates them and enables them to maintain a sense of self-esteem. Dr. Jerry Morton, director of the Center for Alternative Learning, notes that "a lot of very bad things happen to young people outside of the school environment." Traumas at home and in the community often put a student at risk of dropping out and account for many decisions to leave school. From the narrative and emerging-themes data, I will summarize some of the "very bad things" the participants talked about that created emotional stress for them. Although three of the four participants had experienced parental divorce, only one of the three spoke of divorce as a stressful issue. Therefore, I include divorce as a "very bad thing" only for the participant named Delores. Following are the stressors from the wider social context that each participant named.

Pam: a major move from North to South, nonacceptance in a southern school, feelings of not belonging, alienation, poor choice of peer group, learned antischool behavior, unsteady parental control—both parents working, change in relationship with father after the move, truancy, the threat of juvenile detention by school authorities for truancy, illness as excuse for truancy becoming a phobia, low impulse control, poor response to stressful situations.

D. J.: alcoholic mother, drug-using father, fighting between parents (including personal life threats), major move East to West and West to East, cigarette and marijuana use within the home, four different home situations, feelings of rejection by family members, D. J.'s income more important to father than his attendance at school, first-grade retention, grandmother dying of cancer—D. J. becomes her designated caregiver, perceived sexual abuse of mother, believed to be learning disabled in math (but not identified for remedial help).

Iesha: racial slurs because of black identity, white southern mother, black northern father, residence in housing projects, violence as learned behavior, major moves yearly from North to South, first-grade retention, poor speech patterns and resource assignment, depression reported due to the death and killings of friends and family members, 24-hour treatment in mental institution threatened by school authorities that would mean separation from family, teacher prejudice and racist comments, lack of social activities at school because of busing and lack of family resources, gang involvement in the projects.

Delores: divorce of parents, arrest of father by police, rejection by mother at court hearing, stepparent control of and perceived physical abuse toward Delores, early alcohol use, drug use, black males chosen as social group and resulting family tension, family rejection, expulsion from family home, truancy, chronic feigned illness, real sickness not believed by school administrators, fear of pregnancy, desire to leave home at any emotional cost.

The purpose in listing these outside stressors is to make the point that little academic learning can take place when the student is coping with multiple, major emotional stressors. The student's need to preserve self-esteem and survive as an intact person emotionally affected the way in which the student made decisions. Because students were immature, they rarely made decisions based on long-term outcomes. Sometimes, as Pam stated so clearly, the choices were made simply to irritate parents.

HISTORY OF EDUCATION

Now, we enter the mindset of the history of education and the history of trying to identify and explain the phenomenon of "at risk of dropping out." This discussion will link my data to the extensive literature base in regard to "who is to blame: the school, the teacher, or the student?"

A description of an early educational institution known as the subscription school, taken from Kronick and Hargis (1990), follows:

> The subscription school worked this way: A group of parents of school-age children would contribute money for each of their children to employ a teacher to instruct this group of children. The teacher would be required to teach the total age range from 6 to as much as 21. All the students would be in one room, often in a building cooperatively constructed by the same parents . . . . Teachers would work with individual students at whatever level they were capable of performing at and then proceed to the next level when the student demonstrated mastery. Progress was reported to the parents by written accounts describing what the student was learning and what had been mastered. There were no grades of any kind and there was no failure. If there was failure it was that of the teacher. (pp. 15–16)

Because there were "no grades of any kind and there was no failure," it is likely that there was neither competition nor "learning disabled" students. The teacher was expected to teach at the student's ability level, and to justify to parents, in written form, evidence of student progress. The way in which public schools were later organized, with competition for grades on a normal curve continuum, may be responsible for student failure. If a number of students must fail (according to the bell curve) so that a number of students can receive As, then dropping out of school may be a result of the way public education was formalized. Competition for grades, rather than cooperative interaction between teacher and student, results in a meaning perspective that dooms some students to failure. Lack of success at school may be a result of a lack of teaching at school. Student failure is a social construct perpetuated by our public education system.

If we accept the notion that the organization of our schools cannot change, then there are further reasons for the school to accept the responsibility for dropouts and pushouts. The tracking system, which separates students into a college-bound group and "all others," directs major school resources in the form of teacher expertise and technology to the upper track student. The better students are challenged with new learning experiences and taught chemistry, physics, and biology. The lower track students are rarely given access to challenging material of any kind and report boredom as a major factor in their alienation from school. Swadener (1990) challenged this distribution of educational resources with the question "(W)hat if we changed the label 'at risk' to 'gifted' and provided similar enrichment programs, activities, opportunities, and expectation?" (p. 18). She identified graded and competitive school systems as a major flaw in our educational system and made a plea for a nurturing environment in which children are taught by the same teacher for more than one year. She asked that parents as well as teachers and administrators really care about what happens to children at school.

Another crucial issue for students is safety at school. Our tendency is to think of safety in terms of safety from guns, bombs, or drugs, because the news media sensationalizes these issues. My participants were concerned about personal threats in the hallways from bullies, including racial threats as well as physical threats. D. J. described his reluctance to go to the principal and report a physical attack by a bully because of his belief that a complaint would not be taken seriously or in good faith. Once a student was labeled as a troublemaker, his credibility with school authorities limited what he was able to do. We must look at school safety as a concern for the students at the lower end of the pecking order.

Kronick and Hargis (1990) explain that when a grading system was initiated to report student success or failures, teachers began to perceive their role differently. Learning became the responsibility of the student, and teachers were held less responsible for student success in school. Once teachers had presented curricular material, they felt that they had fulfilled their role. It was up to the students to take the initiative for their learning. The idea of teaching and caring for the individual as a whole person appeared to be a concept limited to elementary school programs. Each of the participants in this study felt very strongly that their teachers did not care about them.

A second issue pinpointing teachers at fault, was the specialist system that encouraged the shifting of blame. Teachers as specialists are isolated from each other and from the students. The specialist system monitors numbers—teachers ask, "How many students can I teach in one day or one week?" Often, one teacher is asked to teach as many as 150 students one day and a different 150 the next day. "The specialist system not only encourages shifting blame, it spawns the proliferation of still more specialists and special programs" Kronick and Hargis argue (1990, p. 45). The specialist system allows the teacher to perceive that his or her responsibility is for presentation of course content rather than to the student. In a locked-step curriculum, if a student cannot keep up the pace, for whatever reason, he or she has no recourse for getting special help or consideration. This becomes a major problem to those students with unstable family situations or other major stressors that interfere with learning.

COMPARISON WITH PREVIOUS DISSERTATIONS

In a computer search of recent dissertations, I found three representing "the student voice" about school: one conducted at Harvard in 1988 (Colon-Tarrats); another at Brigham Young in 1989 (Rowley), and a third at the University of California, Berkeley, in 1989 (Epstein). I first summarize the conclusions of the three studies. I then discuss how my study supported their findings. Third, I present issues from my study that appear to be in conflict with previous interpretations.

The Colon-Tarrats (1988) study found exacerbating conditions that put Puerto Rican students at risk to drop out of school were frequent school changes, family problems, and feelings of alienation underscored by teacher actions that were both punitive and inattentive. Rowley (1989) concluded that students bring all their past experiences, including family issues such as parental abuse of children, with them into the classroom. Two major points emerge from that study concerning patterns of early school leaving. The first point is that no student made a decision to drop out of school. Instead, it was a gradual process of increasing truancy, causing a student to get too far behind in academic work. The second point is that the parents of dropouts did not support the truancy of their child, nor did they support the student's dropping out of school. Parents are often unaware of the student's truancy and declining grades until it is too late. The student drops out rather than repeat the grade.

The third study (Epstein, 1989) identified four stressors that predicted failure to complete school: low self-esteem on the part of the student, family problems beyond the scope of the student and beyond the student's ability to cope, alienation from school because of actions of the school staff, and the teaching style of the instructional staff did not take into account the student's personal learning style.

This study supports the assertion that a student carries with him or her all past experiences in school. My findings expand this observation; students bring their meaning perspective as developed by their family experiences and the wider social context as well. A student assigns "meaning" according to the actions and interactions of others and stores the interpretation as symbols in memory. There are key events as well as visual overlays that affect the way in which a student makes choices concerning "school." For those students experiencing major stressors over time, short-term fulfillment of "needs" becomes more important than any long-term educational goal. The retrospective educational life history provided a window of understanding into the meaning perspective of each student and a basis for trying to understand how a student interpreted interaction at school. I would ask that Colon-Tarrats (1988) expand his statement to include not only past educational experiences of each student as emotional baggage but also the wider cultural experiences of each student as it affects his or her choices concerning in-school behaviors. Cultural experience includes frequent school changes, family problems, and alienation in school due to punitive actions by school officials. Inattentive teachers in the classroom and a teaching style in opposition to the student's learning style are issues that can be discussed and monitored if administrators are willing to stop blaming the students..

Could it be that a major area of student anger resulted from major moves across country? It appeared that due to the alienation encountered from a cross-cultural experience, they gained insight into the hidden curriculum of schools. In other words, because of major relocations, they were able to perceive teacher favoritism toward the white, upper social class and to realize that they were not the favored ones. Why they were not the "favorites" was dependent upon how they interpreted past interactions. For example, any time Iesha perceived that she was not accepted socially, her conclusion was that it was due to the fact that she was black. D. J. assumed teachers stereotyped him as a "druggie" because of his long hair. Delores expressed her attraction to black males because they "put her on a pedestal" and that felt like a good place to be. Daddy had obviously taught her what it was like to be put on a pedestal. Pam said in one interview: "I hate money!" This statement made no sense until her anger over Preps and their position of social power was revealed. This position did not arouse anger for Pam when she lived in the North; in the North, she was among the social elite.

Rowley stated that at-risk students lacked social values and a sense of responsibility as illustrated by their poor attendance records at school, their lack of preparedness for classroom learning, and their unwillingness to keep interview appointments. This sounds like the "blame the student syndrome" propounded by public school officials. If a student is learning disabled, the responsibility of teachers and of the school system to teach that student changes. Too often, disruptive students in the classroom are labeled "severely emotionally disturbed," which implies some form of mental incapacity. What about a teacher telling black students to "stay out of her face"? This infuriated Iesha, and she perceived herself to be a leader in changing prejudice that she experienced in school. Does it make Iesha "emotionally disturbed" because her father taught her that people should be judged according to who they are rather than by the color of her skin? From the student narratives, one can see that the conclusions Rowley made are at best shallow and naive to the student perspective.

Since historically there was no such label as dropout or pushout, what was it that took place to get us where we are? When schools implemented grading on the normal curve, some students had to be at the failure end of the normal curve. This is a degrading position for the student, promoting a loss of self-esteem. When the specialist system of teaching was implemented, teachers felt it to be their responsibility to present grade-level material. Should a student be below grade level, the struggle to understand material that was too difficult promoted a loss of self-esteem. If a student moved from one area of the country to another, teacher favoritism became more apparent. The "new kid on the block" is rarely the favored student. Alienation from school came about as a gradual process of not being able to compete academically; loss of interest in school, which led to truancy; as well as experiencing major family stressors beyond the coping capability of the student.

In this chapter I discussed school at fault, teachers at fault, and students at fault and how the mindset concerning education has changed historically. The medical model of blaming the student appears well ingrained within the public school system currently. I then compared my findings with some conclusions made in other doctoral studies in other parts of our nation. Generally, our conclusions were at least parallel.

CHAPTER 7

Review of Student Issues

The students in this study experienced a meaning perspective change from "I like school" to a belief that "School is not for me." Each student was asked questions concerning earliest school memory, favorite teacher, best friend, school attendance, substance use, and other related topics. The students described the key events that changed their attitude toward school as being noncurricular in nature. The key events were experiences outside of school from the wider social context, triggered by events outside of school but reinforced by school interactions, particularly with members of peer groups.

The meaning perspective toward school of each of the four students interviewed for this study can be summarized as follows:

Pam Walker: There was no way for me to get from the position of "outsider" to the position of "insider" after my family moved from the North to the South.

D. J. Whitebear: I learned from my family to be drug dependent before I was old enough to make a logical choice for myself; my family culture and school rules were in conflict.

Iesha Wilson: I am justified in using violent means to react to racial prejudice and racial remarks. I was taught that people are to be accepted for who they are, not judged by the color of their skin.

Delores Cook: I need to feel "special." The only way I have found my "place on the pedestal" is with black males.

For these four participants, outside stressors led to poor grades and truancy from school. The literature on dropouts reports that students are first unable to accomplish the academic assignments, then they begin skipping school, they align themselves with peer groups who are antischool, and they eventually find support for dropping out of school.

The chronology of events the students in this study experienced was described in a different manner. Because high school classes are often lecture courses and noninteractive, the students had time to think about the problems affecting their lives at home. School officials report this emotional trauma on the part of the students as "boredom." When a student begins to withdraw from academic work, we should assume family problems or substance abuse. There are signs that a student needs help when an all-A student begins to fail. There are signs that a student needs help when he simply walks away from school with no precipitating incident and no anger. There are signs a student needs help when she is explosively acting out in a new school situation. There are signs that a student needs help when she skips school and returns only to meet her parents for a ride home. It was documented that even when high school teachers suspected substance abuse, it was often ignored and assumed to be something not very serious.

Should our focus be only on course content, or should we be concerned about the emotional growth of the student as well? Without a stable emotional life, a student will lack the enthusiasm for learning. Elementary teachers assume more of the parent role for their students because of the contained classroom and the needs of little children. For most high school students, the ideal is to help students become independent learners who take responsibility for their own coursework. When this does not happen, we must read a cry for help instead of labeling academic problems "boredom." Too often, poor academic performance is perceived by school authorities to be a student deficit, such as a learning disability.

The students in this study did not follow the typical pattern of dropouts outlined in the academic literature, which starts with an inability to cope with schoolwork, followed by poor grades, followed by truancy that ultimately leads to dropping out. The CAL students described a different pattern: what came first for them was the desire to find a peer group that validated their feelings of alienation and provided recreational escape from overwhelming problems. The fact that the peer groups the students chose were antischool was not what attracted the CAL students to the groups. Significantly, external stress (family and peer-group problems) rather than internal stress (problems at school) set the students in this study on the path that led out of school.

In this study, instead of students not being able to accomplish the curriculum, then getting poor grades—which led to school avoidance and truancy, there was evidence that the association with the antischool peer group was a choice by the participant to find a "place" to vent feelings or to find a "place" simply to have fun and forget about ones problems. This study suggested only the ideal teaching situations. The peer groups taught the student how to skip school and not get caught. Skipping school and fooling authorities became a goal that replaced the goal of academic learning. The truancy then led to poor grades, failure, and expulsion from school.

Does it make any sense to use expulsion from school as punishment for a student who no longer enjoys school and academic learning? Expulsion from school for this type of student may be an asset to the teacher, but it does not help the student. It only supports the student in getting further behind in coursework, which adds to the long-term problem. As D. J. stated, being expelled was like a vacation. And Iesha could not wait to get back to school to "finish the fight."

We, as educators, must find a way to help students under stress define their problems. Once a student can identify his or her stressors, then professionals must help the student make a plan for alleviating the stress.

In our mobile society, a first step might be to organize peer-group counseling at school for students who have recently made a change in schools, for whatever reason, to simply share information about the problems they are facing. This could be as many as thirty students for each adult group leader. The group leader might be generated from a university program in which "student counselors" can receive graduate credit for professional work in the field. The excuse given by schools that dealing with student problems costs too much money is not sufficient, given the number of students experiencing significant stress. If students are unable to learn because of outside stressors, then school officials will have to help students manage stress in their lives if it expects to be successful in serving them.

In the final chapters of this book, we will describe a ten-year effort to serve the individual student from the mindset presented above. When students arrived at the Center for Alternative Learning (CAL), they had already been expelled from school; and their problems had already escalated to the point of involvement with the court and juvenile detention system. CAL dealt with some very angry individuals as well as with families that did not necessarily support school attendance. Our intent is to share basic teaching concepts and strategies learned from the actual experience of building a program to meet the needs of dropouts and pushouts.

Recommendations that can be made resulting from this research are as follows:

1.   Teachers must be better prepared by colleges of education for the cultural diversity they will meet in the field.

2.   Teaching interns (fifth-year students who are teaching in the field) should teach in inner-city classrooms so they can begin to understand the problems associated with poverty that many students experience.

3.   Public-school officials must actively work to eliminate racism and prejudice in the classrooms.

4.   Principals and teachers should be very careful about assigning labels to students, understanding that students' quickly become conflated with the labels authority figures assign to them. Once this happens, a student has little to lose by acting out behavior that the label predicts.

5.   Peer-group counseling is an important school resource. Often students will talk with each other about stressors in their lives much more easily than they will talk with authority figures about these issues. School staff observing peer group counseling can learn what community resources students may need and take action to connect students with appropriate social service or community agencies.

6.   Conflict resolution validates students because it gives them a chance to assert their perspective about disagreements and know that they are heard.

7.   Suspending at-risk students from school is a bankrupt policy. Suspensions only provide at-risk students with unexpected vacation time: they do not experience it as punitive.

8.   Teachers and school authorities must educate themselves about the traumas students experience in their families because of poverty, divorce, physical and sexual abuse, and unemployment. These issues place students at risk of leaving school, which thrusts them into society without the resources they need to succeed.

PART TWO

How a Center for Alternative Learning Operates

CHAPTER 8

The Center for Alternative Learning

Three problems emerge from the literature on dropouts. First, all dropouts are grouped together on the basis of leaving school before high school graduation. The quantitative data loses sight of individual reasons for a student's dropping out. The urban drug pusher who is a dropout is a very different person from the migrant worker or the pregnant, unmarried female; and yet, each may answer on a quantitative survey that "School was not for me." Each dropout is an individual with a unique set of circumstances. A qualitative study could begin to understand a student's perspective of rational and justifiable reasons for disaffection from school.

Second, studies often use data collected by school authorities (i.e., the teachers, administrators, and researchers). Students themselves are never interviewed. Kozol (1992) stated that rarely had anyone other than himself asked students what was wrong with school.

> It occurred to me that we had not been listening much to children in these recent years of "summit conferences" on education, of severe reports and ominous prescriptions. The voices of children, frankly, had been missing from the whole discussion. (p. 5)

This study assumed that the student voice would provide insights from a perspective different from that of educators. The student's truth was accepted as truth; the student became the authority in the process of telling his or her story about school.

Third, we have assumed either that there was something wrong with the student (medical model) or that there was something wrong with the teaching of that student (teacher at fault). Rarely have we viewed the student within a wider social context. Since we know that students do not plan to drop out and that they plan to graduate from high school (Epstein,

1991), perhaps a new mindset is crucial to educators (paradigm shift) in understanding how to meet the needs of the dropout/pushout.

The following categories of dropouts/pushouts (Kronick and Hargis, 1990) will give insight into the type of student referred to CAL for alternative education. A student's response to frustration and failure in school serves as a way to define differing types of dropouts as follows:

1. Quiet dropouts are low-achieving students who experience failure over a period of time, and therefore, simply walk away from school when they attain the age to legally do so.

2. Disruptive dropouts are low-achieving students who act out their frustration at lack of school success. These students are often suspended for long periods of time or are expelled from the public school classroom and are labeled pushouts.

3. High academic achievers who drop out are considered pushouts because they leave out of boredom as well as out of resistance to rigid school rules.

4. In-school dropouts are those students perceived to be nonachievers or minimal achievers without acting-out behaviors.

The disruptive dropouts were those students referred to the Center for Alternative Learning. The center was the brainchild of a small group of educators under the leadership of Dr. Janet Dale (pseudonym), who had previously served as the superintendent of Brook County Schools. She created a grant-supported, nonprofit public school so that senior students who were expelled from the public school classroom could still earn their high school diploma. CAL's board of directors consisted of administrators who were working in or retired from public school systems contracting for services with CAL. In sharing taped interviews about the early years of the school, our intent is to show how the school evolved over a ten-year period and to share information that educators learned in dealing with the dropout/pushout population.

"Nobody seemed to want us." The Center for Alternative Learning had been in existence for seven years when this statement was made by one of the original planners. She described Dr. Dale as persistent in her plan, as superintendent of schools, to provide a place for senior students who were in trouble with the system to complete their high school diploma. Dr. Dale was "a lady interested in the welfare of the students." Ms. Darvy (pseudonym) stated that a catch phrase during the planning phase was, "Pay now or pay later." Dr. Dale believed that if someone would spend a little time and money working with senior students now, it might save society the cost of incarceration later.

In 1980, the school consisted of one room with two teachers and an office that shared space with an elementary school. Ms. Darvy and a counselor, who were consultants to the program, traveled to high schools within the area to inform educators of the existence of a new program that would allow seniors to graduate even if they had been suspended from their high school. From the beginning, there were to be no suspensions from CAL. There were to be consequences for breaking rules, but the mindset was that these students needed help in terms of social interaction within society's rules.

The feeling that "nobody seemed to want us" was a result of the school having to pack up and move every two years. Ms. Darvy also commented that in her thirty-five-year involvement in education, her CAL position was the only one in which she was fired every June and rehired every August. In its seven-year history, the CAL director was never given a budget by school systems contracting with CAL to serve some of their students until mid-July. Therefore, the teachers, counselors, and classroom assistants never knew from one year to the next whether they would or would not have employment. In the early years, the teachers were paid less than regular public education classroom teachers.

From the beginning, the idea behind the program was to have a limited class size with a classroom assistant and counselor serving each room. Early in the fall of each year, class numbers might be as small as three or five. As the year progressed, the numbers always increased until each of four classrooms exceeded the limit of fifteen students. By the end of the school year, there was always a list of students waiting to be admitted. The seniors who earned enough credit for graduation went back to their original high school and graduated with their class. Usually, CAL also had an end-of-the-year ceremony for those completing graduation requirements as well as an assembly to acknowledge the personal accomplishments of each student for that year. Sometimes the accomplishments were small, but staff celebrated each student's success with great pride.

Ms. Darvy was responsible for planning curriculum and instruction for the program. She was not the director. The director she spoke of in 1987 was Dr. Jerome Morton, who believed in behavior modification for students as well as staff. "Jerry stretched people to be the best they could be," Ms. Darvy asserted. Dr. Morton directed the center from December of 1985 until August of 1991.

The following interview concerned goals and organizational structure as perceived by Dr. Morton. All teacher, counselor, and assistant names are pseudonyms.

RK: Talk to me about goals for the center. Did those change over the years?

JM: When I first came in December of '85, the most immediate goal was to help the staff develop a positive behavioral management system. . . . I also wanted them to be more involved in a participatory management style. Another goal at that time, the program appeared to be about to end. It had no viable source of income. It had no strong support from either of the two school systems. At that time, it was no longer getting support in terms of grants. Contingent upon survival, I felt, was improving our existing staff to be much more positive with the kids, which I thought would show more and bring about more dramatic results, expanding the program so it was large enough to make an impact. And another goal that I had was to formalize and expand upon the community agencies and organizations involved with the alternative center.

RK: How big was CAL in '85?

JM: I think there were three classrooms.

RK: So how did those goals change? Were the goals the same last year or—

JM: Well, the goals became more sophisticated, more specific. . . . Everybody basically was implementing the token positive reinforcement economy [described in detail in Chapter 16]. And everybody could articulate it fairly accurately. Not everybody was implementing it appropriately. Part of my feeling was that people had to learn, that you couldn't expect them all to have the same base knowledge in acquired skills. . . . If we had the luxury of looking for a position for a year or so, then we might have found people who had more on-line skills. . . . Instead, what we did was we got people who had a good heart and had some skills; and we would want to develop these skills within them.

The next goal was to bring staff together more—*to work better as a team.* The next goal that I had at the start of last year was moving into more individualized instruction and tying in better every activity.

RK: I am interested in the strategies that the center uses that could be transferable into the public (school) classroom.

JM: Clearly, *the positive behavioral management approach, the valuing of the child, and the focusing on the child's strengths* and not investing a whole lot of energy in the shortcomings of the child, which means you intervene in such a way that it is a learning experience for the child as opposed to a punishing, revengeful kind of process. I see that as a major flaw in public education right now; the implied conceptualization, that if the child is a rule breaker, if the child does something that is culturally offensive, then we must utilize punishing revenge on the child as opposed to *seeing what this child hasn't understood and hasn't resolved* in their own feelings with successful ways of expressing them in interacting with people. So if they have encountered an injustice, they can change it. Or if once they understand the situation was not an injustice at all, then they can change their own perceptual set. . . . If you [CAL] can do it with the most hostile [students] to the system, think what can happen with people who are responsive and predisposed to value what the system does with them! [Interviewer's emphasis]

Dr. Morton's immediate goal in 1985 was "to help the staff develop a positive behavioral management system." Time was taken each week for a meeting that every staff member was expected to attend. After finalizing school business, one staff person became the focus for positive feedback. Dr. Morton expected the staff to interact with positive feedback 80% of the time. This meant that every day we practiced saying what the student was doing right before there was criticism. The critique could be positively framed by saying, "You did this, and this, and this correctly, but let me show you how you can do this a little better." We, as teachers, rarely have been expected to use this model in public school.

In our staff meetings, each of us shared with the person of the day what we believed were his or her greatest strengths while working with these special kids. For some, it was academic skills; for others it was establishing a family atmosphere of support. Staff practicing weekly with each other the search for the best in each member helped to reinforce the practice of continuously informing each student of what they did well. The director expected us to ignore bad behavior as much as possible and to constantly issue positive reinforcement for the slightest behavioral change. Once a teacher began to practice this model, it became evident how often other teachers get into the pattern of saying, "This is not good enough, do it over," without providing the help and support that is needed by some students.

The students at the center were social misfits at best and juvenile criminals at worst. They came to the center in emotional distress, unable to identify their problems, and incapable of finding solutions. A quick overview of the type of student the center was serving in 1985 will demonstrate the change in population over a five-year period. This information was part of an unpublished article written by Dr. Morton entitled "An Alternative School Program for High-Risk Adolescents."

Descriptive data about CAL's students include the following: thirty percent are actively involved with juvenile court, twenty-five percent live in group-home type settings, thirty-five percent receive psychological counseling from some other agency, seventy percent receive services from other agencies, forty percent are on a subsidized lunch program, ninety percent report having difficulty following school rules, sixty percent failed at least one grade, seventy percent of the girls have been sexually assaulted, forty-five percent report using drugs sometimes, ten percent are intellectually gifted, fifteen percent are gifted or talented in an art area, and fifty percent are handicapped [according to P.L. 94-142].

Often, when the students arrived at CAL, they were shut down emotionally. When asked to make an academic choice, they would respond, "I don't care, it makes no difference." They were unable to see that making a decision one way or another could bring about a different outcome. They had given up on making decisions concerning their life because their perception was that any decision was out of their control. Adults imposed their meaning perspective and rules upon teenagers to show them who was boss; and at the same time, adults expected teenagers to move toward autonomous adulthood.

The most important position that CAL took with these students was to express loudly and clearly that every human being has worth; that every human being can make one's place within society; and that in order to make one's place, one must be aware of the choices one makes and the outcome that is contingent upon those choices. The next most important position of CAL was that the emotional trauma from which the student was suffering had to be dealt with before the learning process could begin again. Each person's basic needs had to be met. These students felt alone and unloved.

A loving environment was established at the center. This was accomplished through Dr. Morton's willingness to promote each staff member's highest capabilities and strengths. Each classroom took on the essence of the teacher's strengths as if it were a stable family; *each classroom had a different personality.* While this might have been perceived by an outsider as a weakness, we perceived it to be a strength. If a student were very immature, and maybe even slow, he or she would be assigned to Ms. Strauss. Ms. Strauss had the patience of Job. She was in the process of acquiring stronger academic teaching skills. Her classroom actually had created a living room space with sofa, chairs, and a rug. The counselor for that classroom was particularly adept in identifying major emotional problems and making social service connections for the student as well as for the family or responsible adult. Students in her classroom were outside family normalcy as we know it.

JM: That was one of the real transformations that I saw . . . in allowing the growth of a staff person. Strauss's class, she is one who has changed a great deal. She was extremely indecisive, always asked other people what they thought about a situation and did what they thought instead of what she thought. This last year she was the best person in dealing with the most serious emotionally disturbed kinds of kids. She . . . did not get knocked off balance very much . . . which wasn't the case when I first knew her. Major change there! Had a nice balance between promoting the social interactive skills and the academic stuff.

Her counselor played the role of stepping in and making decisions for

Ms. Strauss, with the goal of once she began making decisions, backing off and supporting her in her decisions. The counselor had a little bit of difficulty backing off as Ms. Strauss took on responsibility for her own decision making. But she came forward and pressed the issue and gained knowledge with just extreme skill. The guidance counselor . . . has a sense of humanity and vision of a mission in terms of impact on culture, takes great personal interest in the young people, and tries to constantly reinforce them.

The teacher assistant in that class was an extremely strong personality, spontaneous, happy, willing to articulate her views, but also willing to listen to other people's views. That provided a real nice balance there.

I presented Ms. Strauss's classroom as the nurturing classroom for immature or highly emotionally disturbed youngsters. At the opposite extreme was Ms. Fine's room, where academics for college preparation were stressed. Several students in her room were taking college-credit classes at the local university as they completed their high school accreditation. The students in Ms. Fine's class were given freedom of choice in terms of planning their academic day.

JM: Ms. Fine's class is very much oriented toward academic responsibility, meeting those responsibilities before any play! She moves the kids, she is a good organizer, understands the sequential learning process of shaping things for kids. She is strongly independent, does not like to be pushed or forced to do something. Will react negatively to a situation and then once she reflects on it, will change her position or accept divergent positions or situations. Will engage kids in social activities. [She] is very consistent in her rewarding processes, but the social activities are secondary to the academic.

Her guidance counselor is very, very logical and works best when dealing with explaining consequences of behaviors, and providing information that is necessary for the young people to acquire. Has difficulty in establishing close emotional relationships with kids. But does in her own mind establish close relationships to the point that she will go to great lengths to correct an injustice or to pave the way for things to work smoothly for a child.

The teaching assistant, the way I first saw her was as a very angry human being. [She] felt that her talents were ignored . . . felt that she was denied an education, in [lack of] opportunities by the system. [In contrast], last year she was initiating activities, sponsoring boys clubs, feeling confident in herself to ask other staff members to do things. And they did do them. *Went from being primarily negative in how she interacted with kids to being primarily positive, supportive.* That was one of the real transformations that I saw . . . in allowing the growth of a staff person. She just really, really has changed over that period of time.

One student in Ms. Fine's class who was highly capable academically shared with me how angry she became when a substitute teacher demanded that she write in her personal journal before beginning her algebra. The student had arrived at school with a plan for algebra first thing in the morning when her mind was fresh. She became highly agitated and disruptive when the substitute teacher's plan was imposed upon her. Here was an only child who was used to having things her own way. She made all of her own decisions; she had worked since she was fifteen and was holding her fifth job in the real world. For someone living an independent life and resisting authority on a regular basis, dealing with the substitute teacher for one day was a major issue. And major issues for this student became reason enough to walk out of the building, knowing full well that this was cause for dismissal from this program. She probably knew that "Mom" would use her influence to later readmit her. Mom appeared to be a major component of this spoiled-child syndrome. Rarely do students become assigned to the center without family "baggage" attending with them. As Ms. Darvy stated, "The counselors spend as much time counseling family members as they do counseling the student."

Ms. Fine's classroom focus was around social activities and group interaction. The team worked hard on developing a sense of responsibility on the part of the students.

JM: Ms. Fine, another classroom teacher, has a tremendous ability to develop loyalty within the student and a sense of commitment in responsibility on the student's part toward the teacher. In turn, the teacher and the teaching team has a sense of responsibility and loyalty toward the student. This is extremely good in engaging the students in projects and social activities in group work. She is extremely talented in doing that. She had difficulty in keeping the children academically focused and [in] tying the social activities to the academic. Had difficulty on being consistent. Her counselor provided a good anchoring point for her.

The counselor is extremely good in group interaction, on getting in the middle of it, letting go of the trappings of authority, but just getting right down with the kids and working with them. She has a tendency to get too emotionally involved with people and that makes her vulnerable for accusations that she has crossed a boundary of being professional and [being too much the] personal friend of the student. But her orientation and Ms. Fine's orientation toward social activities merged well.

The teaching assistant also has a predisposition toward dealing with social things. She is somewhat confrontational in expressing her personal opinions, which is a behavioral pattern that is long ingrained and that she is very proud of. She is undereducated and doesn't understand things expressed in philosophical kinds of issues. Needs them explained in very concrete and specific ways through situations with children. Her

personality tends to be very rigid and so rather than invest a lot of energy in
trying to reshape some major characteristics of how she interacts with the
world, it's a wiser use of energy to take the way she deals with the world
and match her up with kids who deal with the world that way.

Each classroom had a personality; each team had a personality. The
director attempted to place a student according to that student's needs. At
one time, the center had tried the practice of changing classes as in regular
junior high school, only to discover that the one-room schoolhouse, family-
atmosphere system served the needs of these children better. These students
were weak in positive social skills; those skills needed to be taught along
with the academic skills. Remaining within the same room and interacting
with the same staff persons daily were major factors in the student's
success. If a student felt that his or her room assignment did not "fit," the
director would make changes only after a lengthy trial period of
adjustment. A change of classroom assignment happened only rarely. The
mindset of the school was that the student needed to be aware of the need
for social-skill development in order to adjust to new group situations.
Always, this was discussed with these teenagers in terms of real-life
experience and preparation for holding a position later. When I asked one
of my students what his goal for future employment was, he answered,
"My parent receives a monthly check from the federal government and I
assume that I will too." We must be aware of such an assumption and
change the mindset to one of productive employment for these students.

Sizer (1992) believes in real-life training similar to that described
above. As Ms. Darvy stated, "Not all students are college bound; in fact,
not all students will graduate from high school." Sizer states the following:

> The real world demands collaboration, the collective solving of problems. . . .
> Learning to get along, to function effectively in a group, is essential. Evidence
> and experience also strongly suggest that an individual's personal learning is
> enhanced by collaborative effort. The act of sharing ideas, of having to put one's
> own views clearly to others, of finding defensible compromises and conclusions,
> is in itself educative. (p. 89)

The one-room-schoolhouse concept provided the opportunity for the
staff to hold each person responsible and accountable within a group
setting. A student story illustrates the director's expectations of both
students and staff. Our center had a female janitor who did her job well:
she took pride in her work. At the end of one school day, as Judy was
mopping outside the counselors' offices, a student came running down the

hallway and with force, pushed the mop handle protruding from the mop bucket. A large amount of water splashed onto the floor.

As the student left the building, Judy began wringing out the mop preparing to mop up the puddle. The director intervened, telling her that, although he appreciated her willingness to do so, it was not her responsibility to clean up the water. The cleanup would be Jerry's responsibility. He then followed the student out the door of the school.

The student was standing in the gravel parking lot beside the exit, along with two staff members and several other students from his group home. They were awaiting their ride by van to the group home. The director pleasantly approached the student and asked him to return and clean up the water. The student vigorously cursed the director, refusing his request and working himself into an agitated state. The director, still speaking in a calm voice, repeated his request, adding that he realized that the student did not intentionally spill the water. It was simply an unexpected consequence of the push on the mop handle, but someone still needed to clean up the water. It did not seem fair to ask Judy to do it since she had worked hard all day; it was time for her to go home to her family.

The director went on to explain that the student did not have to clean up the spilled water; he was simply explaining the situation to the student. It was an accident that the student did not intend to have happen. Someone needed to clean up the water and the director was perfectly willing to mop it up. He was simply providing the student with the opportunity for responsible action. The director did not want the student to be punished nor did he want the student to risk missing his ride home.

With that said, the director returned to the school hallway and the water on the floor. The director began wringing the mop as a first step in cleaning up the mess. Unexpectedly, he felt a gentle tap on his shoulder. Looking up, he met the student's gaze. No words were exchanged. The student simply took the mop handle and began mopping the floor. When the mop was full of water, the student placed its head in the mop wringer. The director reached for the handle; the student let him take it as he proceeded to wring it out. Once the mop was ready, the director handed the mop back to the student. This process was repeated several times.

When the floor was cleared of water, the director broke the silence with a quiet, "Thank you." The student smiled, turned, and ran down the hallway and out of the building. A lesson about life and personal responsibility for one's actions was in place. Public school staff members and students can be made aware that we learn from our mistakes when there are valid expectations from leaders!

In its seventh year of existence, CAL was housed in another school building near a subsidized housing project. The building was shared with a nursery-school program that served the projects. Fear was expressed by the community that these "teenage criminals" might hurt the small children. This prompted CAL to ensure that the preschool program director and the community knew the rules the school had for managing the students' behavior—no CAL student could leave the classroom unattended; no student was allowed to smoke, nor were they allowed to drink; and no screw-top bottles were allowed in the building.

These students came to us addicted to nicotine, to alcohol, and sometimes to hard drugs. We existed in a neighborhood in which drug deals and prostitution took place within view of the classrooms. Our job was to seek outside professional help for student addictions and to have stated consequences that would be imposed if the student was in violation of the rules. One student described what it was like to be addicted to nicotine and to try to concentrate on academic work when he needed a smoke. He stated that he was sure his teacher would allow him to use the bathroom, knowing full well that he needed a cigarette. On the day the director caught him smoking in the men's room, the director said, "Son, no one enjoys cleaning a bathroom. But you are aware of the consequences for sneaking a cigarette in here. I expect you to thoroughly clean two urinals before you leave school today."

As the student began to protest, the director began cleaning two adjacent urinals. He emphasized the safety precautions both of them must follow so that they would not get sick; he did not want the student to become ill. After thoroughly cleaning the two urinals, the director turned the cleaning tools over to the student. Without protest, the student accepted the cleaning materials and began the task. The director left the bathroom. When he returned, the student's two urinals were as clean as those the director had cleaned. Without fanfare, the director thanked the student. The two rewashed their hands, shook hands, and nothing more was said. Regular public school officials would have suspended the student for smoking.

To suspend potential dropouts from school for any reason makes no sense at all. Getting students to become aware of what is causing their problems, acknowledging that the problem exists, seeking help for the student, and providing support during the process from a responsible adult makes sense. The problem sometimes was finding the responsible adult. One of the students who was an admitted "druggie" had family members who were dealing in drugs on a regular basis. When families have a different moral code than that of the public school system, the student is caught in the middle.

Not only was it important for the director to match the incoming student to the teaching and counseling staff, but it was also important to match teacher, counselor, and teaching assistant strengths and weaknesses to produce a working team. Another point to be made is that the school grew by using trial-and-error methods. We, as staff, were asked to learn from our mistakes just as we asked students to learn from theirs. This required a constant process of reflection and collaboration, a continual effort on our part to believe in ourselves and in the expertise we were building. The following statements of the assistant director explains the process of building a program:

AD: Any new program in terms of concepts has to have implementation. And I think we were short in knowing how to implement because we had never worked with these kinds [of kids]. And the only way that you can gain experience with these children is to work [with them]. You don't receive that from universities. You don't receive that from books. You receive that by practical every day getting in here and having the experience. I don't think anything that I did in college prepared me to work at CAL. There were certain skills that I had in counseling that were helpful, and in a lot of ways, probably helped toward my being a success here. But I don't feel that there were a lot of things that I learned from a university standpoint that were really instrumental in teaching me to deal with [these] children. I think that came from the practical side of implementing a program before.

RK: What do you see as practical professional knowledge that can be used in a public school classroom?

AD: I think we need to concentrate a good deal of the curriculum on a tough area to cover: on self-esteem, on developing children's self-esteem. If anything saddens me in education at this point it is that *sometimes teachers are real destructive with children's self-esteem.* Instead of building I think we tear it down. I think we tear it down and we are not consciously aware of that. I think that one of the things we have to realize is that we are role models in everything we do.

RK: If somebody didn't know anything about this school and you said that a student tested you . . . can you think of any concrete examples?

AD: [Laughs] For example, you go into a classroom and a student is in a pretty antagonistic kind of mood. And that probably, in all reality, has nothing to do with you. The other thing, I am going back to the first question because it ties in with this one. Universities need to *teach teachers to depersonalize* some of the things that are going on in education. You know, because kids are angry, and come across as being angry, it doesn't mean that you are the source of that anger. . . . Because most of the time you can help the kid work through that and then the kid says, "Gee, I am really sorry I caused ———. I really don't feel that way about you. I really didn't mean to say that. I wasn't angry at you at all." When a child begins to see you truly as a human being, then he begins to feel as though he can relate to you. . . . If I don't know anything else, I do know this after nine years: *Kids respond to nurturing.*

She concluded her interview by stating that there is no easy answer for working with this population, nor is there any single answer.

CHAPTER 9

Engaging Students With Art

Have you ever faced a blank canvas or an empty piece of white paper, knowing that you were expected to create an art project? Suddenly, your mind is an empty slate. Your life-long experiences as well as an infinite number of daily landscapes and still-life images disappear in an instant's notice. What should you do?

Suddenly, the way in which you tackle life's daily problems becomes your "approach to task" in solving this one. If you are a quitter in life, you will look at the blank white surface. As you stare at the emptiness with no ideas in your brain, your mind will defend your position by saying, "You can't do this, no need to try. Just walk away from it and forget it!"

However, if someone has taught you to take a large task and break it down into smaller, doable tasks, you will begin using a cognitive process something like this: "I know I must not leave any white of the paper unused. Therefore, I will mix a beautiful paint color with the intent of covering the entire area of the canvas and calling it a 'ground,' that is, the background. I can do that. Just get started with the most beautiful and pleasing color to me that I am able to mix. I can then choose to paint the ground with gusto: wide and lively strokes exhibiting a variety of value changes (darks and lights). All I need to think about is creating a surface color and texture that interests me. Chances are, if the painting interests me, it will in some way be pleasing to my viewer. If I consider this start to be a failure, I can always paint over this first attempt and tell myself that I am building a textural groundwork. Simply by painting over my first attempt, I give myself a second chance."

Simply getting started and becoming personally involved in the task may suggest the next step of the process. It is too early to plan a final product; the journey has just begun. Placing the paint with gusto begins to involve my conscious mind as well as my hand in the process. The conscious mind begins to ask itself, "What if this?" and "What if that?" My mind automatically takes over in trying to solve the problem at hand. If the canvas suddenly becomes "too precious," I can free myself from its constraints by turning the canvas upside down and taking control. I make the choices here; I am in control.

My primary purpose here is to make the reader aware of the parallels with life choices: One can either live life by avoiding problems or by being challenged by problems. After becoming personally involved with the initial draft, the artist has completed an integral part of the creative process. Furthermore, this personal involvement may trigger the next step of the process. To make a conscious plan to just get started by doing a simple and enjoyable task first that leads to solving more complex problems later is an approach to life. In the art room, it involves a sense of trust that there will be help and support during a process that may be a new experience.

Approaching a new task is a cognitive process that involves at least three steps. The first step is to gather the material necessary to begin the project. Gathering art materials (the canvas, paints, brushes, and sponges) or writing materials (paper, pencil or pen, eraser) prepares one to be creative and creates a mindset in which work can begin. I like to remind students that once they have completed this step, they have already begun the work.

The second step, gathering ideas, is a more complex endeavor. This step involves gathering data in a variety of ways in order to move the project forward. This may be accomplished by actual work on the piece (painting a ground color to see what it looks like or generating a first draft of a written piece) or by research (finding written material about the subject of the piece). Talking with relatives and friends about the subject may be helpful as well. Each of these activities may help to generate a plan of action for the artistic or academic project.

The third step is output, or producing the product. The three-step creative process that students learn in art class is the same process they will use to complete academic work. Once students successfully complete the process in one venue, their confidence grows so they can do the same process in another venue. Additionally, teachers can learn much about how students think by observing their work process in art class. Knowing at which stage in the process each student needs extra support will assist the student to acquire a life-long skill that will enable them to solve problems by making a plan.

My very first attempt at painting more than thirty years ago was on a long, narrow board, using acrylic paint. My favorite color is a peachy-pink. I began to mix red and yellow together on the board, rather than on a palette. The grain of the board along with the mixture of yellow and red created, almost without my help, a beautiful sunset reflected in the clouds of the sky. I was so taken by something that I felt I recognized from deep inside that I simply added some telephone poles and lines using perspective that created distance (like railroad tracks that disappear into a point on the horizon) and called it complete. I remember this event clearly; the experience was very meaningful.

I took the painting to show my friend. She, too, became excited. To her, it was a Kansas sunset from her childhood memories. She spoke of her longing for open prairies and a landscape unencumbered by trees and mountains. My friend may still have that little piece of wood hanging on a wall somewhere. I have not seen it in years. And yet, the image of that painting, as well as the choices I made that affected the final outcome, burned sharply into my visual memory. My vision of both the process and the product appears crystal clear to this day, thirty years later!

My approach to painting has not changed very much over the years. Today, I might begin with an idea, either an idea of my own or an assignment from my teacher. My mind is faced with many decisions. Which art form will best express my idea? What do I wish to say? Shall I draw using paper and pencil? Will it be "soft," as in a rubbing, or will it be "textural," using sharp slash marks? It could be a combination of the two. Infinite numbers of choices are possible. Not only does the plan involve gathering of materials, but it also predetermines decisions that will affect the way the finished product looks. An idea supports my work now; whereas, in the past, simple abstraction, using color, texture, and form, sustained the process.

A thought process involves making comparisons, such as soft versus hard line or textural line versus all-over shading. These choices are requirements if I choose to add color in the form of chalk, pastels, or colored pencils. My choice of papers, whether shiny or textured, colored or white, as well as the weight of the paper itself, will affect the outcome. The mind is immediately full of questions that demand choice, and choice is determined by visualizing an anticipated outcome through a cognitive means known as compare and contrast. If I want "softness," then I might choose pastels on a nontextured background color. A watercolor wash is also a means of attaining a soft and flowing picture. The artist, desiring a hard-edge painting, would use an entirely different choice of tools, paper, and outcome. A canvas demands an entirely different plan and thought process.

Why are these thought processes so important? A parent might say, "I'm afraid if my son or daughter takes art that the teacher will try to make an artist out of him or her. And the life of an artist in our culture is not the lifestyle I want my child directed toward!" And I would reply that the thinking skills just described can be taught. Visualization, making choices by means of comparison, and the sequencing of ideas are thought processes used by upper level business managers, architects, lawyers; all are highly successful college graduates. The teaching of art inevitably allows us to experience and discuss the thinking and learning process.

The process of art allows us to see the world in which we live from a different perspective. Once a student is asked to paint a sky, he or she will never see the sky in the same way again. Once a student is asked to re-create a textural surface, texture in nature and everyday living will never go unnoticed again. The more one is asked to create or re-create, the more observant one must become to the details of life. The act of creating art supports a reflective process. The process often lends itself to appreciation of life rather than to a denigration of life. Creating art should express the artist's feelings about the subject matter. How often do we stop to monitor our own feelings? How often do we express those feelings to others? How often do we reflect?

Art is a means of connecting ourselves to our emotions: fear, joy, isolation, anger. When I worked with at-risk students, I could "read" their paintings and gather important information about their feelings of "place" within the world at that moment. Students at risk of dropping out of school are often troubled by many elements of stress in their lives. Black is frequently their color of choice. Left alone to express their emotions on canvas, they paint very sharp angular forms. The composition of their work is chaotic; anyone could read the confusion. It is important for these students to express these dark and ugly feelings.

My rule in the art classroom was that each painting had to be completed before another could be initiated. In honesty, I told the students that art materials were very expensive; therefore, I could never justify their tearing up even one piece of paper in anger. The students always learned more by not giving up. My real rationale for this policy was that rarely had anyone ever challenged these students to follow through on their responsibility to complete a task.

These students were so shut down emotionally that when I asked them to make those initial choices of paintings versus drawings, canvas versus paper, paint versus chalk or pastel, they would expect me to make the choice for them. When given the opportunity to be in control for once, they would bypass any decision making. I never made this initial choice for the art student. Sometimes I became exhausted with the waiting time. Sometimes they became very uncomfortable in their resistance to make a decision. When they became uncomfortable enough, they would decide. Once the art piece was their decision, it was their responsibility to complete it. I believe I taught many more life skills than art skills. The art process can be used to teach students with low self-esteem that the decisions they make affect the outcome they get.

Let us return to the description of student art in which black paint and sharp objects abounded. At the same time that I asked students to express their feelings in paint, I began to teach them that art is a universal language and that they, too, could begin to read art. As they painted their black, gloomy, graffiti-type work, I would show them examples of simple, abstract, quality art. I asked them to label each piece in terms of summer, fall, winter, and spring. We first talked about the colors typical in spring and in Brookton, Tennessee. This was an easy season for them to describe: pink, light yellow, spring green. Fall colors were as easy as winter. Then we talked about the feelings we experience with each passing season and began to integrate these ideas with color. Gradually, over time, each student began to believe that there was a "language" to art. Once they accepted this truth, they could then use the language they were building to produce more meaning within their own work. The colors in their paintings began to brighten.

Art is a process of learning a symbolic language of color, shape, size, perspective, and other concepts. Art is a process of reflecting on one's life and experiences. Art is a process of connecting with one's feelings and of expressing those feelings symbolically so that a viewer can read what the artist has to say. For the teacher, art is a means of understanding a student's meaning perspective about solving problems.

Now that I have shared my meaning perspective or belief system about teaching art, I will describe my experience of teaching art in an alternative high school. These students were considered to be hard core. Many were under court order to attend or else be incarcerated. For most, this was a last opportunity for a public education.

My definition of art is any creative endeavor in which a student tries to express himself or herself, whether that expression be poetry, drawing, writing, drama, painting, pottery, or photography. My definition is more process oriented than product oriented. One can use creativity in writing history papers or social studies papers or use creativity to think about new ways of solving math problems. My openness in defining art allowed for many choices during the planning process. For instance, a student choosing painting needed to decide on whether to do realistic or abstract painting, whether to use watercolor or canvas, what color combinations to use, what technique to use, and so forth. Making choices about something demands a thought process of making comparisons and making decisions. A student can then predict or visualize an outcome based on that decision. Too often we tell students what they must do and exactly how they are to do it. By usurping their responsibility, we take much of the thinking process out of the preparation and planning. We say we believe in freedom of choice, and then we take all of the freedom away.

I often tell the story of comparing my mother's child-raising techniques to those of the mother of my childhood friend. I had certain after-school responsibilities that my mother expected of me whether she was at home or not when I returned from school. I was expected to know what to do and to take the responsibility to do it and to think for myself within some parameters that were already established. My friend, on the other hand, was met by written notes everywhere when her mother was not present. Precise instructions for what was expected of my friend were written out: "Change out of your school clothes and into play clothes first. Your after-school snack for today is wrapped and waiting for you in the refrigerator. You are not to leave the yard until I return at 4:00 p.m. You should set the table for four people for dinner. You can wait until after dinner to do your homework."

I remember thinking that my friend's mother loved her daughter more than mother loved me: I envied all of that caring and planning written down for my friend to follow. With maturity comes a different perspective. How much thinking was expected of my friend compared to the trust that was placed in me and the sense of responsibility for myself that I acquired? Yes, I made mistakes in growing up and in becoming responsible, but I was expected to learn from my mistakes. My parents taught me responsibility for living in the real world.

The education classroom should provide a learning atmosphere in which students make choices, make mistakes, learn from mistakes, and become involved in the learning process. Making mistakes and learning from those mistakes prepares students for real life.

The key ingredient for engaging students in the process of art, I discovered, was expecting a student to complete a process before making assessments about the quality of the work. I asked students to complete a task before they judged its quality and content because everyone assumes that they should be able to "do art" whether they have ever had any instruction or not. We do not assume that one can read without instruction, but the students often assume that they should be able to create quality art work without previous instruction.

Keeping one's judgment out of the creative process is an impossible request, but what I was trying to avoid were the many false starts of at-risk students that waste art materials. I negotiated a verbal agreement "up front," based on the high cost of materials. Then, I was consistent with every student in terms of the agreement. There were times when students would prematurely call a work completed in order to crumple it up in front of me, throwing it with rage into the waste can. I allowed that because art can be most frustrating at the beginning. One must meet oneself in the process. One has unrealistic expectations and must endure feelings of failure to meet these unrealistic expectations.

Art, then, was viewed as a process of lowering the students' false expectations while increasing their skill-building abilities. I mediated to help students cope with feelings of inadequacy and to help with the art process. I took these tasks very seriously. From my perspective, it was a matter of the student's educational life. My intent was to give a student a window through which he or she could view his or her approach to a task at hand. Invariably, the at-risk student would avoid making even simple choices. The standard initial response was, "I don't care." I refused to give in to this attitude, never making the decision for the student. I helped students come to a decision by giving them more information about art processes, but I never made the decision for them.

I remember well D. J.'s process of learning to write. D. J. was "shut down." He would barely talk to me, let alone perform any task. He decided, finally, to write his autobiography in the form of a praise poem (praise poems are described in Chapter 10). The assignment was to choose someone important in your life and tell his or her story. D. J. chose himself. I took this as a very good sign!

D. J. refused to put pencil to paper. I convinced D. J. that I was interested in his ideas, his thought process, and his memory, not in his English skills per se. We negotiated an understanding by which he would tell his story and I would "play secretary." But there is a bit of the devil in me: I used no punctuation. That was his job.

I then read his words back to him with no pause for sentence structure. When all of the words and ideas ran together, we talked about where he expected me to pause and take a breath. Ah ha! He became aware of a need for periods and capital letters. A rationale for the use of punctuation was discovered! We went through a similar process to justify paragraphs and indentation. It was not long before D. J. was doing all of this for himself on a computer. Spell check was a godsend for this student.

I discovered during the process that this hard-core dropout "druggie" had great ideas and had developed a highly creative mind. He had long been creating poetry for songs that he could sing from memory. D. J. continued writing poetry for years after he left the alternative school. I would like to believe that some of the skills he learned in art class that he was able to transfer to academic work were partially responsible for his success in earning his GED diploma. He arrived at CAL with no self-esteem and no self-confidence; he left the center with a belief that he could solve problems that he encountered.

I would also place a postscript here. Once a sense of trust was established between the two of us, D. J. came to me for help in math. I came up with the perfect plan for understanding fractions, percentages, and decimals, all three of which challenged him. We used the U.S. monetary system, which D. J. already understood. Parts-per-hundred parts was taught as a thinking concept. As he held a dime in his hand, we wrote 10 cents, 1/10, .10, and 10%. He could see that if 10 dimes made a dollar, then 1/10 of $1.00 equaled 10¢. We practiced math using a convention with which he was already familiar. We tied his learning to something he already knew and understood. A highly creative, visual learner, he, when able to manipulate the money in his hand and tie it to his real-life experience of monetary exchange, had a window of understanding that made math a usable concept. This is an example of what Dr. Morton means when he asks that teachers tie outside activities to academic learning.

D. J. eventually "cleaned up his act." He quit using drugs because he decided for himself to use his brain, and he understood that drugs compromised his ability to do that. D. J. made some productive decisions about his life. He stopped blaming his family-life circumstances for his lack of skills and began to set his own educational goals. After he stopped using drugs and earned his GED, he entered a two-year college in another state. He supported himself and did above-average work in college.

CHAPTER 10

Visiting Artists Program

I described the alternative-center students as deviant and at risk of dropping out of school. Public school officials believed that truancy was the major problem; yet drug and alcohol abuse, illegal use of weapons, and teen pregnancy were stated as major problems by the students themselves. A study of CAL by Kershaw and Blank (1993), *Student and Educator Perceptions of the Impact of an Alternative School Structure*, identified the students as "disenfranchised" and "marginalized." These students were pushed out of the traditional public school classroom by teachers and administrators, who sometimes perceived CAL as a "valuable place to 'get rid of students' who are causing excessive problems." No wonder then that these students are reported to have poor self-esteem and to lack a sense of self-efficacy or self-competence.

We applied to the Tennessee Arts Commission for a grant to bring visiting artists into our program. Our perception was that artists see themselves as marginalized in society, on the outside, looking in. We felt that our students would relate to artists both in terms of the art presented and in terms of the perception of being on the fringes of society. I asked each artist to represent his or her work as evolving. Often artists work with one idea, assessing, analyzing, and then creating a similar work at a higher level. I wanted students to understand that simply doing work one time does not constitute the highest level of achievement that can be attained. Getting ideas on paper and then revising one, two, and maybe three times toward a better product is a standard procedure for many artists.

Our teachers were open, flexible, and interested in innovative practices. One of our first visiting artists was Laura Hawkins from Theatre Troupe Central, a company of national renown anchored in Brookton. I remember Laura's first visit to CAL. She was in the later stages of pregnancy, dressed in costume for storytelling, packing a guitar on her back for song embellishment to the stories she told. I also remember the students' response to Laura Hawkins. They hugged the walls of the classroom whether standing or sitting, enjoying the entertainment as long as they were not asked to participate. There was eye contact between some who asked, "Just what is going on here?" The ever-present fear of many students was that they would be chosen to do something that would draw attention to themselves. Laura had come to begin a program of creative drama, and the students were terrified.

Laura perceived these students to be shut down emotionally, as I, also, did. When I asked my art students if they would rather draw or paint, they invariably responded, "I don't care" or "It doesn't matter." How was Laura supposed to develop a creative drama program for students who would not communicate? These students were either ignored within their home situation or they were confronted by powerful adults about their behaviors in a manner that triggered defensive and angry responses. In Laura's personal notes to herself at that time, she writes:

> The student needs to learn to think and problem solve.
> The student needs to share his thoughts and conclusions effectively, both verbally and in writing.
> The student needs to develop a frame of mind not to take all information at face value.
> The student needs to develop strategies to verify and substantiate information.

She said that creative drama and theater arts are about communication and that creative drama is neither subject dependent nor is it content dependent; the process helps the student to own his or her behavior and his or her choices. She used improvisation around current events after she perceived that the students were comfortable with improvisation. How did she get students comfortable with creative drama techniques? She began with the voice. She did an entire series of exercises about getting the muscles of the diaphragm to support sound. Through games and classroom interaction, she managed to get students to release sounds from their bodies in a way that a stage artist must do in order to perform.

As soon as the voices were in place, she began to use body language. She encouraged the use of mime in which students in one group prepared a small action skit for another group to interpret. The students created the ability to visualize an assigned object and to communicate meaning to another group of students without the use of words. The artist's intent was to use the creative drama process in the classroom to develop social-interaction skills and basic communication skills. Relationships are built on shared experience. The workshops were about being able, being empowered to "do" anything, being empowered to finish an exercise or to imagine. The exercises taught students to think, to question, to make decisions, to interact socially.

Laura wrote in her notes at the time:

> I believe what happened here at CAL in the past was that these students weren't challenged in certain areas. There weren't expectations for them to achieve as writers. They were bored with academics in their base schools and brought that attitude with them [to CAL]. Some children don't fit well into the traditional academic structure; but when released to a process like creative drama, they generate all kinds of energy. The rules don't fit their own behavior. [One must] channel their interests towards specific objectives. Once they are working towards those objectives and when those objectives are generated from within themselves, they are on task.
>
> Say we're going to write down some of what we've been doing, just write it down, and we're going to learn how to write a draft. *Get the ideas on paper.* I don't care how you spell it! Try to have it so that you recognize what you meant when you go back to look at it. Just do it. Get it on paper. That's why people make dictionaries, erasers, and computer spell-check programs. That also gives us an opportunity to learn to use resource materials. What this does is create a need for these technical tools for the writing processes.

Laura Hawkins began in a concrete manner with voice and body exercises similar to those a kindergarten teacher might use to teach five-year-olds. When students are so shut down emotionally and verbally, one must begin the communication process from the beginning, never assuming that all students are creative or that they will be comfortable with this process without an initiation. Some of Ms. Hawkins' written rules to herself concerning these students were:

> We will warm people up physically using simultaneous activity so that no one is the focus, no one feels self-conscious. It's not risky; we are in a safe place. Maybe we can work in pairs. It's a good time to play a tape; you can move to the music if you want to.

Her next step in the process of getting students comfortable with performance was to play a game called "Follow the Follower" from Spolin (1986). The students moved toward watching and listening to the other person, getting feedback, paying attention and following, giving, and taking. Students were asked to bodily create a mirror image of his or her partner. The partner may have been gesturing with the right hand, but to do a mirror of that gesture, the student needed to use his or her left hand. As students created the bodily image of their partners, Laura played music that she frequently changed—to something staccato, or something very flowy and pastoral, or something contemporary, like rap. The music changed the students' attitudes and emotions about what they were doing. They needed to learn to share emotion and to demonstrate that emotion with a particular person with whom they had established a rapport.

Once the students had learned to mirror each other physically, we introduced exercises to help them learn how to mirror each other verbally. Each of the activities drew the students more and more into focus because each activity required that a student had to pay more specific attention to the person with whom he or she was working. They were establishing a rapport and learning to play off each other. We then took the exercises a step further and gave the students a script called "Please/no." We asked them to explore all the various ways in which they could say please and no to each other. We asked them to observe vocal variations and inflection. In the process of doing these progressive exercises, the students were building a set of skills that prepared them to be performers.

Learning activities prepared the students academically, almost without their knowledge. Laura introduced a history game that she called "Your Momma." Each student studied generations of women in his or her family. Students were given a variety of categories to research about each generation of women—education, clothing, technology, and so forth. Students used traditional resources like history books or encyclopedias to learn about the categories, but they also used nontraditional resources. Many of them spoke with their grandparents to learn about their experiences in order to complete the assignment. Students particularly liked researching the history of women's fashion. As they participated in the game, they learned about U.S. social history.

Laura Hawkins also developed a geography game with them in which they assumed that each group of students had recently won a lottery of $10,000 with which they were to plan a trip of their choice around the world. As the students planned their itinerary, they studied world maps, the monetary system and exchange rate for each country, and the climate and the type of clothing they might need for each country. They used travel guides, banks, and travel agencies as sources of information. They argued with each other about the rationale for airplane stops along the way to their final destination.

One can see how many decisions and choices would have to be made in planning a major trip for a group of students. What language is spoken in each country? What are the rates of bed and breakfast inns compared to hotel rates? Should the group remain in each place long enough to see the historic sights or should the group hit only the high spots?

The classroom teacher could easily inform the visiting artist as to the curriculum content she needed to cover. When the students could imagine and create a trip of their own around the world, the motivation for learning became intrinsic. Positive social interaction began in the classroom but quickly extended to the real world outside as contacts were made to actual agencies. When a former director stated that some teachers had problems relating field trips and social activities to the classroom curriculum, he had an activity such as this in mind. The students visited travel agents and banks and talked to community persons as they gathered information about the countries they selected.

Laura Hawkins enjoyed a year-long residency that allowed for building student skills over a period of time. But several other storytellers and writers who came for short-term residencies could build on some of the skills Laura had instilled in the students.

A second writer who achieved successful social interaction with the students was Renee Saunders. At the time, Renee was finishing a Ph.D. in education at the local university and was, therefore, able to develop the latest teaching techniques in our classrooms.

Renee Saunders distributed a handout on the first day of her workshop that articulated a philosophy of how to build writing skills that parallels my own philosophy about doing art:

THE WRITING EXPERIENCE AND PROCESS

Writing begins with ideas that can be put down on paper. These ideas don't have to be well thought out or believable. They just have to come to you. Or you can make them up. The idea can be a thought, feeling, emotion, memory, fantasy, or reaction to something real or make believe. The difference between writers and the millions of people who say they are writers is that writers write down what they think about, feel, or what comes to them; others just think it and wish they would write it down.

Writing begins with the first word on paper. Don't think that you have to have your idea in its final form or polished for a publisher or something. *Just write something down.*

At first, don't worry about grammar or if it doesn't seem to be correct. Just write something down. You can correct it later in a rewrite. Or maybe you might decide that the way you have written it is the way you want to tell the story. It might be your style.

WHERE DO I BEGIN?

Begin wherever you want to begin. The best stuff is stuff you are familiar with—your life. You are an expert in one area for sure, and that is your own life!

WRITING IS *POWER*!

You may want to start with an event, or you may want to make up something. You can change stuff around, or you can tell it as it happened. Again, you are the expert in your life.

WRITING AS HEALING AND GROWING

Sometimes writing can open doors or close doors. Sometimes writing can bring to the surface some memories or things that you might not have even thought were there, or remembered ever happened. This can be good, but it can also be uncomfortable. If it is uncomfortable, then you might want to share your writing with someone else and talk about it. It is amazing how healing writing can be when it is used to put something down and to let go of it. It is wonderful when it happens this way. But sometimes this can be uncomfortable at first. I cry a lot when I write because some of the things I write about are sad stories. I live with my characters and I hurt with them. But they do more for me than I do for them. They help free me and, I hope, free some of the people who read my work. Don't be afraid of writing if you think it will be painful. Chances are it is more painful not to write, to hold it in and let it control you, than to write about it and see it in a different light.

Renee then spoke of journal writing as a good starting place and discussed poetry, short stories, novels, and screenplays. She ended her handout by repeating, "Write! Just do it!"

Two other visiting artists conducted writing workshops for our students. Anna Dixon, also from Theatre Troupe Central, introduced praise poems. She described how family histories have been maintained in Africa through the telling of praise poems. She began by discussing *Roots,* the television miniseries about slavery and the separation of families.

As her introduction to the students, Anna first performed two praise poems, one from a play and another that she had written about her own family history. She used rhythm instruments to accompany her voice. She discussed with the students possibilities of subjects for praise poems: heroes, places, things, situations, and especially students' personal histories. The praise poem at the beginning of D. J. Whitebear's chapter (Chapter 2) was written during Anna's workshop.

Her goals and objectives were as follows:

To introduce students to an art form (praise poetry) with which they are probably not familiar.

To introduce or add to students' knowledge of another culture.

To spur students to correlate their own culture and personal history with the culture and history being presented.

To activate students' creativity by having them attempt to commemorate their own history or culture in the manner of the art form presented. In other words, students should write praise poems.

To initiate students in the art of speaking in front of a group as they will do when sharing their poetry.

To educate and entertain students with the art of storytelling.

And finally, to instill students with a sense of excellence and a desire to achieve their own excellence, no matter what the vehicle.

Often these artists began by sharing their own work, getting students excited about writing possibilities, and then asking for some simple initial writing samples that students could revise.

A third writer, Miss Ruth, began by sharing her poetry about common, everyday things in her life: old shoes, her dogs, and even her grandmother's funeral. Miss Ruth's poems were written with a sense of humor that had a little twist, similar to the following piece:

DOGS

I always have strays.
They find me. Or arrange it so I find them
in a nonreturnable sort of way.

Some are subtle, like Rusty.
He came in summer and just sat down in the plastic pool.
There's a limit to how long a 75-pound, wet,
bushy dog can be ignored in a small wading pool.
Eventually I had to notice.

But the best technique was Dolce's.
One spring day I was planting flower seeds by the chain-link fence.
Nothing existed but the dirt and the digging, the flower seeds, and me.
I don't know how long it was before
I felt uncomfortable.
Something else had come into my world.
Uninvited.

I looked up and saw her on the other side of the fence,
watching me, waiting.

"No, not yet," I said out loud.
"I'm not ready."
Tears began to trickle down my face.
"Rusty hasn't been dead long enough."

But, even as I spoke,
I knew I had no choice.
Dolce had chosen her human.

Inspired to share some family secrets that may have been hidden for some time, the students were able to write some unusual works, such as the one that follows:

> The best time was also the worst time because my Dad shared something with me I will never forget.
> My Dad was in and out of jail all the time. The day before, my Dad had been shot in a hold-up. He got put in the hospital.
> My Dad shared with me, "Do not live the life I have lived," he said. He was sorry for not giving me a better time. He gave me a cross that his Dad had given him.
> "Son, keep this in your heart."
> "Dad, I will," I said. "Dad, I will miss you."
> "I love you," he answered.
> "I love you, too, Dad."
> That night he died. That was the worst day.
> The week after, I got adopted by a good family that loved me. So those were the worst and the best days.

And another, this one written by a fourteen-year-old girl:

BECAUSE . . . .

I love myself

> because I know there's no one like me
> because I'm special as I can be
> because I am very unique
> because somehow I'm petite

I love myself

> because I'm confused
> because I think that I'm going to cry
> because I am weird
> because it's hard for me to lie

I love myself

because I have two sons
because I know my life has just begun
because I want to be free
because I love to be me

In Miss Ruth's notes concerning her objectives for the residency, she wrote the following:

> The objective of my residency was to help students recognize their individual experiences as valid and valuable resources. The focus was more on content of the writing than on mechanics.
>
> I offered several ideal options based on people/places/things and the students responded in writing. Since our maximum time together was three 45-minute sessions, I opted to spend most of that time actually writing. I found the wee small gems to be eloquent testimony to the effectiveness of brevity and simplicity in writing as an art form.

In addition to the creative-writing artists who visited CAL, artists working in a variety of other media also came to the center. Three sculptors, representing different aspects of the three-dimensional arts, interacted with the students. One young man who did environmental art taught the students how to collaborate on a plan of action and how to work together as a team. The group built an outdoor dome of sticks that was large enough for the entire group to enter at one time. As it was an outdoor project, the students were particularly motivated to complete this project. A second artist, whose theme was lobsters, did not interact as much as she explained her thinking processes and rationale for the value she found in doing her work. The students were interactive in terms of their questions and their challenges to her about the worth of this type of art. A third sculptor was a Cherokee Indian who was handcarving a very large totem from a large tree. This artist had been commissioned by the state to create a piece that would be placed in a roadside park along the Trail of Tears. The Trail of Tears is the name given by Cherokee people to the trail used during their forced removal by the U.S. government from the southeastern United States to what is now Oklahoma in 1838. Thousands of Cherokee people died during the journey, and many survivors experienced cultural dislocation and tribal divisions for generations to come. Because of this interaction, a small group of CAL students completed a totem of their own made of clay. Each student chose an animal to represent himself or herself and devised a method to attach their animal to the animals of other students. A journalist from the local newspaper came and photographed the completed totem on the same day that a group of Native Americans visited our school to share their culture of being connected to the earth.

Other visiting artists included a storyteller, a musician (who played Mississippi blues and Appalachian folk music), a painter of canvas paintings, an actor, a drummer (who taught students how to make a drum like his). Each artist brought to the students a dimension of understanding of an art and why people commit to doing art. I am afraid there was a real fear on the part of the parents that emphasis on the arts fostered a play time rather than a learning time. However, the students often understood the relationship between their lives and their approach to art.

The following is a student writing project done in the style of a praise poem:

> Greetings everyone.
> This is a story I've got to tell about Art.
> Art is a way of releasing anger.
> There are different types of Art.
> The one I'm going to talk about is painting.
> The thing about painting is you go by strokes and more strokes.
> When I do art work it takes time for me to get it all together.
> And get it right and looking good.
> I thank Rosa and all my family
> For giving me encouragement to do more art.

Two more examples of student work follow, as they describe the experience of the visiting drummer:

> There was a man who came yesterday to our school who taught us how to play drums. He was funny plus he was fun to be with. We saw him twice and we got to play his drums. He taught us how to make the drums. He uses skin from deer and wood, glue, rope, metal rings, and strings to make his drums.

This previous example may not look like much until you understand that Billy was one of our youngest students, emotionally disturbed, and somewhat mentally challenged; and he experienced great difficulty expressing himself. His short piece of writing is next to a miracle.

> D   is for different and dazzling.
> R   is for regal and rightness dude.
> U   is for ultimate and unison.
> M   is for mellow and maximum bass.

The student artwork was often angry and bitter, but it was crucial that we not criticize the efforts that were the beginnings of opening up to feelings that often were misunderstood. I admit that when we had our student show, I had to get a faculty consensus on what works might offend the viewing audience and give the program a bad reputation. Some works were held back from the exhibition, providing an opportunity to teach students about the appropriate use of body language and verbal language in pieces created for public audiences. The following work represents a very angry student and his personal justification for some violent acts against society. When I was aware of this much anger in either the paintings or written works, I was able to go directly to the student's counselor for advice and collaboration on the best methods of teaching that student.

Here is the work, which very well could be lyrics from a rap song. I chose to accept it as a personal work:

Searching for an answer you'll never find
An answer from reaction, a chemical reaction
Then you're blue in the face as you try to state your case.
You can think with your ———, but it can't shout
Don't even try to understand what the hell is going on
I can't imagine how the example got so far gone
You chauvinists say you want a state
I'll give you a state, a state of unconscious!
Retribution, no solution, constitution
Discrimination throughout the nation, reining hatred
Against the system we must rebel
I refuse to live in your hell
I am what you fear
I am the truth
Live your life
Take someone else's
The real world's outside your door
Don't even try to tell me what you think is right
When to you Blacks are Niggers
And Jews are Kikes
You expect to be taken seriously
But your actions are more than curiously
And our language you hate
And you don't even know why you feel this way
Cause daddy hated this and mommy hated that
Difference and you always in frustration
Taking out a violent nature
You're so full of hate, so full of hate
You kill a man, and it's a natural fate
Why the hell do you hate?

Because society had been cruel to them and they had nothing to lose, the students often challenged the thinking of their teachers and mentors. Judges were ready to put them either in juvenile detention or in jail; teachers were ready to get them out of the classroom, whatever that meant; administrators were more than willing to send them to an alternative situation to get them "straightened out." But the artists were more understanding of what it means to live on the fringes of society. In fact, in general, most of the artists felt that their residencies had been a challenging experience. One artist articulated this sense after her time at the center:

> I wish to thank Rosa Kennedy for inviting me to share my gifts with the students at the Center for Alternative Learning. I wish to thank the faculty and staff at the center for their support. And most of all, I wish to thank the beautiful young people of CAL for their willingness to open themselves to a stranger in a very special way. I not only saw students grow, I grew. I not only saw students learn about writing, I learned about writing. Because of my experience with the students and the process that we all entered into openly, I am a better writer. And for that, I am most grateful to all the students and the Center for Alternative Learning. With much gratitude,
> —Renee Saunders, Writer—

CHAPTER 11

Strategies for Teaching Dropouts

The CAL staff shared a vision that we could turn students' lives around. Our students were in trouble with schools, and many had been court-ordered to attend our program or go to jail. We knew that if we could give students a successful experience in school and help them to acknowledge their success, we would be well on the way to reengaging them in a learning process.

We assumed that students were given work to accomplish in public school that they were incapable of doing. Therefore, we began with an individual education program (IEP) for every student as though each was a special education student. We might have a student who was performing at second-grade level in math and at tenth-grade level in English. Although it seems logical that teachers would be sensitive to the abilities of their students when they assign work, they are sometimes, for several reasons, not able to meet the needs of individual students who have fallen behind. First, the tracking system places students on an educational path that moves forward inexorably. The goal of this curriculum is to cover mandated material rather than to monitor the ability of students to process new material. Second, the daily class changes for each subject a student takes allows some students to fall through the cracks. Teachers may not be aware that a basic set of skills is missing in an individual student unless they talk to each other about the student. Students feel that when they lack the basic skills needed to accomplish an academic task, it is the responsibility of the teacher to teach them how to do the task. Teachers feel that their job is to present the lesson and that it is up to the student to accomplish the task, or at the very least, to seek help. This is the root of the problem. This fundamental disagreement exists between teachers and students about the process of education.

The CAL staff knew that the students needed to have an experience of academic success and that that success needed to be acknowledged. High school students who could do only second-grade math were guided through second-grade-level work. A teacher never assigned work without making certain that the student understood how to go about accomplishing the task.

This seems so basic. But because of sheer numbers of students that each high school teacher sees each hour, students who lack basic skills get lost in the system. The most frequent comment from at-risk students about public school teachers was that they showed favoritism. Teacher favoritism results when some students acquire the social skills that a business expects from its workers. Those students coming from business-oriented families or from academic families have a far greater advantage in our public school system than do those students coming from poverty-stricken homes. Although this seems obvious and logical, many educators have not given adequate consideration to the obstacles to learning that students who are deficient in social skills encounter when they enter public school classrooms.

Feuerstein (1979), in his book entitled *The Dynamic Assessment of Retarded Performers*, cites case study after case study of teenage students referred to him for assessment who had the potential for learning and the potential for remediation. He speaks often of cultural deprivation. If cultural deprivation can happen within a middle or upper income family as described by Feuerstein, think of the home life of students with one parent working many hours each day or of students who live with grandparents or with family members who are alcoholics. It becomes incumbent upon the schools to teach the social skills necessary for a student to learn from a teacher. Yet teachers expect that students should come to school having learned these skills within the family. Some families are sick. Feuerstein described one set of parents who had survived the concentration camps in Germany during World War II, had lost spouses and children, found each other, married, and had more children; but the home life continued to be depressed. These factors affect the learning potential of children.

We know that emotional well-being affects learning. We know that basic biological needs must be met. We know that by the time a student enters middle school, a certain set of basic skills should be intact, including social skills and academic skills. We know that when there are stressors in the student's life as a result of his or her family life, we cannot change the family (under normal conditions). What we can do is talk to the student in an effort to discover what the problem is. We can also do curriculum-based assessment to establish the student's grade level for each subject. We can expect positive social interaction from the student and begin an exchange that teaches positive exchange. We can use behavior modification so that we give positive reinforcement when we approve of the behavior and ignore behavior that does not serve the student's educational process. We can implement the use of reflective journals in which teachers or counselors expect students to write about incidents as they happen. The intent is for the student to gain insight into his or her behavior and, as a result, to continually set new and realistic goals for more positive actions.

This sounds easy and logical until you meet with a highly resistant student who may feel that negative attention from the teacher or peers is better than no attention at all. Such a student may clown in the classroom, show disrespect for the teacher, or use improper language at school. Students with low self-esteem do not believe that compliments are sincere when they are given. Change is a slow process. For those children lacking positive social interactive skills, *accepting a compliment from another must be taught.* The center provided time for group work during which paying compliments and accepting compliments could be practiced.

Our staff was highly valued, especially by each other. *The licensed professional counselors* available to the students were also available to the staff. How often do we concern ourselves with the mental health of teachers? We knew that we worked in a highly stressful situation every day. Some days we simply needed a day of rest and relaxation to regain our momentum. We were given R and R days over and above any accrued sick days, and we covered for each other. For at-risk students, this is a good modeling technique. We did not expect that we or they would be perfect, but together we would monitor and modify behavior over time.

Students were never suspended from school for mistakes that they made. They were *expected to learn from their mistakes.* Does it make any sense at all to suspend a student from school when school is the last place on earth that the student wants to be? How illogical can we be?

We had a time-out room within the school. The student could be directed to this room as a "cool-down" tactic. The student was expected to come to the room with an academic assignment but was not required to do academic work while in the time-out room. Time out was strictly there for the student to regain self-control and to think through any episode that had taken place. The student could request time with his or her counselor in order *to gain a perspective on the confrontation.* The student was expected to reflect on the action he or she had taken and, as the student grew in confidence and self-esteem, to converse with the other party and to apologize for an outburst if possible. These *adult behaviors had to be practiced and acquired over time.* Without an adult expectation that the student could act in an adult way, no progress would be made. *Unified adult expectation* among teachers, teacher assistant, counselors, and the director was the intent. Adult behavior was expected.

The following strategies and teaching/counseling interventions review some of the major points presented in previous chapters of this book. The vision of the staff at the center was that strategies that worked for at-risk students were highly usable for all students. All students respond quickly to positive reinforcement when it is sincere. Students learn that their good work is recognized, and they are open to listening to ways in which the work can be made better. Through this process, they learn to trust that the teacher cares about their learning process. This principle is at the heart of the positive reinforcement model.

Students must be given challenging work and the support to accomplish the task. Student are then helped to acknowledge success in the smallest increments. Acknowledged small successes lead to greater risk taking and greater future success. Following are the strategies and interventions to be utilized by all teachers:

1. Set student academic and social goals that are *realistic goals.* (M-team entrance to the program).

2. Prepare an IEP for every student: Identify where the student's work is below grade level and get remedial help to attain grade-level expertise. IEPs are valuable as tools only when the student participates in drawing up his or her individual plan—and only when the plan is implemented. In addition to the IEP, curriculum-based assessment (CBA) can be implemented by any teacher anywhere.

3. Use a positive reinforcement behavior management system based upon Bailey and Morton's (1970) RAID model (Rules, Approval, Ignore, Disapproval).

a. RULES: Rules that are stated in a positive manner are developed within each classroom and clearly displayed for all to see.

b. APPROVAL: Eighty percent of all evaluative statements to students should be made in a positive manner. Positive communications include the use of verbal communication, nonverbal communication, tokens, and predetermined rewards.

c. IGNORE: Inappropriate behavior of one student is ignored as much as possible. Appropriate behavior desired of that student will be praised when observed in a fellow classmate as soon as possible after the errant behavior has taken place.

d. DISAPPROVAL: Disapproval will be initiated immediately when there is danger of physical injury, destruction of property, or significant disruption of the learning process. The inability to earn a privilege is the primary consequence of disapproval (Bailey & Morton, 1970).

4.   Place the incoming student into a "contained" classroom that will best suit the student's needs, a classroom that "feels" like family. It is possible for each school to create one self-contained classroom with the goal of creating a stable social group for emotionally needy students. The recommendation includes having professional staff available for individual and peer-group counseling. This supports the integration of the new student into the classroom family.

5.   Provide a safe environment for the student to vent his or her anger. This is usually done through one-on-one counseling or within a peer-group counseling session.

6.   Use self-management so that teachers as certified professionals have a voice in what happens in terms of school policy.

7.   Encourage an awareness by administrators that teaching at-risk students is a high-stress job and that *each teacher's mental health is of utmost importance.*

8.   Ensure that the incoming student understands the contract under which he or she enters the program.

9.   Believe that each student's intent is "noble" from that student's meaning perspective. This means respecting the dignity and worth of each individual and treating him or her with kindness, understanding, and equity.

10.   As the school perceives the need, connect students and their families to social services in place within the community. This may include placement within a group home to provide a safe living place for the designated student or help in dealing with problems concerning drug use, alcohol use, sexual abuse, or pregnancy.

11.   Provide help and support to each individual's unique set and combination of problems and circumstances. There is no one right answer or even a packet of answers. There are strategies and interventions; but the teachers must use their experience, creativity, professionalism, and, most of all, trial-and-error tactics while reflecting with other teachers in the program about how best to serve any particular student. Each individual has a unique set and combination of problems.

12.   Help the student develop self-esteem by acknowledging every small success, whether academic or behavioral. In order for this to happen, a student must be met where he or she is so that every gain is significant and named and acknowledged. This demands that the *process* of changing behavior be as important as the *product* of learning.

13.   Realize that teachers are role models in everything they do and that at-risk students are experts in reading inconsistent behavior. This means that a teacher cannot say that he or she cares about the student without acting out that caring behavior on a daily basis.

14.   Practice the depersonalization of critical language used by an angry student in school. The anger is directed at a system that the student perceives to be unfair, punitive, and revengeful, and not at the teacher.

15.   Relate to students more as individuals and as people rather than as the teacher in charge or the authority figure. Students who begin to see their teachers as human beings find it easier to relate to them. Beginning to acknowledge that you, the teacher, are really there to help is a major step in personal student growth.

16.   Nurture and care for the student. Young people respond to nurturing.

17.   Understand that the belief system of the student at risk is likely to be antischool and antiauthority.

18.   Begin to establish a sense of trust.

19.   Discuss learning disabilities with the student. Talk about what a learning disability is. Ask, "Do you know what this means? How do you feel about this?" Talk about psychological testing and what that means in language the student can understand.

20.   Use interventions and methods available through special education resources for special-needs students.

21.   Perform as the licensed professional teacher that you are, demanding a voice in the educational process of your students, especially those at risk.

22.   Acknowledge and tend to your own personal stress.

23.   Create a sense of unity and belonging for each student.

24.   Realize that highly mobile families create students who feel like "misplaced persons."

25.   Accept the fact that some children are potentially dangerous to themselves and to others. These children need a secure facility whether they are using chemicals or because they are potentially violent. They do not belong in an alternative center.

26.   Accept that a student's family problems may be extreme.

27.   Teach the student strategies for dealing with other people in the world.

28.   Understand that teaching skills for positive social interaction may be as important initially for students at risk as academic skills. Many CAL students were able to acquire jobs (that is, their skill levels were adequate);

few had the skills needed to keep jobs because their social skills were inadequate.

29.   Support other teachers in their efforts to reach difficult students. Collaborate and brainstorm about innovative ways to reach and teach the problem students.

30.   Use reflective journals as a means of documenting new approaches in trial-and-error tactics to reach difficult students.

31.   Encourage the use of journal writing by students as a means of documenting goals accomplished and setting new goals.

32.   Never back a student into a corner: Always provide an avenue out of a confrontation that allows the student to save face.

33.   Try to minimize the potential embarrassment of anyone, especially in a group activity.

34.   Use conflict resolution to get all sides of an issue on the table and out in the open.

35.   Anticipate conflict between students or between teacher and student, and be prepared to mediate before the conflict escalates. Being one step ahead of the action is an intervention technique based on timing that is learned only through practice.

36.   Use the time-out room to separate students in confrontation. CAL students perceived this to be an opportunity to gain control over their behavior rather than as a punitive action. Immediate counseling and listening tactics provide a means for the student to understand the conflict in an effort toward interacting in a more adult and positive behavior. This helps students learn from their mistakes.

37.   Genuinely care about the student, even if you disapprove of his or her immediate behavior.

38.   Be willing to listen to a point of view and meaning perspective different from your own.

39.   Do not assume that middle- to upper-middle SES students are free of problems great enough to "shut them down" to the learning process. All students have problems that are perceived by them to be unmanageable at times.

40.   Seek out colleagues as listeners to help deal with difficult problems, whether student based or personally based.

41.   Believe that you can help a student at risk become a productive citizen.

During an interviewing process, I asked the assistant director of CAL, who was also a licensed professional counselor, to role play the part of an incoming student. In this excerpt from my interview with the assistant director, she articulated the meaning perspective of a typical student newly arrived at CAL:

AD: When I say I am frustrated, I am angry because I can't do something that everybody else can do. And it appears to be easy for them and difficult for me. And I feel sort of lost in a way. Feel like I am not going to make it. Nobody else in my family has made it. I want to make it, but chances are I may not.

A lot of times I can't control my anger. I just feel like I want to explode, and there is no one there that I can seek out and help me work through that.

Labels (such as dyslexic) make me feel dumb more than anything else. All I know is that I don't learn like other people do, but teachers have not bothered to tell me what my label means. Maybe I am retarded or really stupid.

Speaking about student behavior, she said the following:

AD: If a student is acting out his/her frustrations in some way, the student must learn the skills of being able to control the behavior and to modify that behavior because the world either accepts them or rejects them based on their behavior.

I need to teach him/her strategies for dealing with other people. I need to teach how to interact more positively. The way I teach the student to interact more positively is to be a proper role model and to model behaviors that I want to see the student able to implement.

As educators, we must prepare for a future of more rather than fewer students at risk of school failure. One third of the nation's thirteen-year-olds say that they use illicit drugs. Only half of the parent population reports only moderate involvement in their child's secondary education. A ten-year study (Carey, 1998) reports that adolescents between ten and fourteen years of age could become "lifelong casualties" of drug and alcohol abuse, teenage pregnancy, AIDS, violence, and suicide. The study concludes that adolescence is a time of neglect.

Teachers can be the change agents of the future, an idea presented in Fullan's (1994) book, *Change Forces.* He believes that educators must be encouraged to acknowledge the punitive and revengeful means of dealing with students in distress. All teachers are encouraged to perceive the acting-out behavior as a cry for help, to depersonalize the angry speech and action against the system, and to realize that these cries often emanate from the wider social context. School can create a stable, family-like support system for students who feel alone.

My intent is that every classroom teacher can use the strategies and interventions stated above. Each school, or at least each school system, could implement one self-contained classroom with a professional staff to nurture and support with compassion some of the students who would otherwise be suspended from public education at a time when they need nurturing most.

PART THREE

How to Create a School for Emotional Healing

How to Create a School for Emotional Health

CHAPTER 12

Introduction to Administrative Concepts

Many factors must be considered when creating and maintaining a school designed to promote the emotional healing of damaged children. The factors are all interconnected. Fortunately, the school does not have to be perfect in implementing all of them. However, the school must make progress in implementing a significant portion of them. The major anchor of the program must be its philosophical orientation. The various components of the program must be continuously reviewed in light of the philosophy of the school. When discrepancies are found between the philosophical position of the school and practices of the school's staff, something has to change. Either the program component or the philosophy of the school must change so that the school is working to create an *ever increasing consistency between what it says it does and what it actually does.* This consistency is extremely important to the young people in the school. The one thing that all of the students have in common is the inconsistent ways that they have been treated by adults and institutions.

Whether the philosophy of the school is described as a mission statement, a belief system, or a goal, it needs to reflect a *valuing of each student as an important person whose underlying motivation is positive.* There is no denying that young people often make errors in interpretation of situations and, therefore, errors in judgment. There are consequences to be faced as a result of those errors. However, there is a clear distinction between someone making a mistake or misinterpreting a situation and someone who is bad by intent. School staff who believe that someone made a mistake in the way he or she chose to correct a perceived injustice can positively assist the student to find a correct interpretation of the situation or to find good solutions to use in resolving the problem. School staff who believe the student is a bad person and that is the cause of the bad behavior are predisposed to use punishment as a primary tool to bring about desired behavior changes. *Helping students find positive ways to correct perceived or real injustices done to them is a healing process.* Punishing students for inappropriate behavior does not promote emotional healing. Most often it has the opposite effect.

Once a philosophy of the school that promotes healing has been established, a framework exists by which the other components can be addressed. One parameter that needs to be established early in the school's development is the kind of students it intends to serve. The age range of the students, the degree of behaviorally and emotionally troubled youth it can serve, and the resources it has to bring to bear are all key elements in determining how the school for healing will function. A school that focuses on early-elementary-school-aged children will be quite different from one focused on adolescents. Seventh through twelfth graders are the focus of this writing.

Adolescence is a time for young people to begin to establish themselves as independent adults, to learn how to become appropriately sexually responsive persons, to establish their own value systems they will live by as adults, and to join society as productive and active members. It is natural that young people will make mistakes during this process. We expect toddlers to fall a lot before they learn to walk with skill. Because toddlers are small, adults find them relatively easy to control by simply imposing their size and strength. Adolescents are much more difficult to control. The size and power of their bodies seriously limit the amount of physical control adults can force on them. The adolescents must actively desire to follow the controlling directives of adults. The authoritative adults have to use different strategies and intellectual conceptualizations with the adolescents than they use with young children.

The typical school for healing teaches at-risk students who have problems of varying magnitude. They would not be at the school for healing unless they had already experienced serious difficulties in the public school environment, and they bring those behaviors with them as they enter the alternative school. They sometimes refuse to follow critical directions given to them by school authority figures; they will challenge authority figures; they are prone to openly violate rules of behavior; they argue frequently with others, using abusive and socially unacceptable language; they aggressively try to impose their will on others; they are prone to get into fights with others; they refuse to do much of their schoolwork in or out of the classroom; they are frequently tardy and absent for no clear reason; and they exhibit behaviors that are irritating to those trying to follow established social customs.

The targeted students will follow the directions of adult authority figures most of the time, provided it is given in a nonthreatening manner; although the directions may have to be given several times before they comply.

Their noncompliant behaviors are typically manifested by leaving the situation when directed to stay, refusing to cooperate, or arguing about issues for extended periods of time. *They often challenge the thinking of the authority figure.*

Students may be prone to violent outbursts, which are usually verbal in nature. Students may have a history of physical fighting, but they are not considered to be dangerous to the physical well-being of others except through accidents in judgment during the heat of the moment. It is apparent from the personal histories of the students that far too many of them have had very bad things happen to them. For most at-risk students, the trauma from these experiences has not been successfully resolved.

Students admitted to the school for healing are intellectually capable of learning. Most of them have failed to acquire an education—both an education that is appropriate for their age level (as defined by evaluative tools in the public school system) and an education that reflects their intellectual capabilities. While many of the students may have diagnosable learning disabilities or other disabling conditions that require special modification of the way they receive educational instruction or communicate what they have learned, they are capable of learning.

At-risk students are usually social isolates. They do not participate in extracurricular activities. Their few friends are like themselves and tend to be known as troublemakers in the regular school program and in society at large. Because of their lack of social interaction skills, they tend to be shadowy figures that one never quite sees at typical gathering places, such as at the shopping mall or at school, unless they are in confrontational situations. It is hard for the general population to get to know them. Many of them have experimented with the drug culture. However, their own use of drugs has not caused them to be in altered states of consciousness for long periods.

Psychotic individuals, significantly brain-damaged individuals (genetic, trauma, or drug induced), physically dangerous individuals, or individuals who will not follow the majority of the directions given them need to be in a more controlled environment than the one to be described. Healing environments for those individuals can be designed utilizing many of the principles and strategies of the healing school. Those environments will have to have specific components designed to meet the very special needs of their targeted populations.

The underlying principles that are recommended for the school for healing apply to all settings. It could be argued that if staff in the regular school environment utilized them, there would be no dysfunctional children. The intellectual argument falls prey to the realities of today's society. Certain students in the regular school program elicit behavior so disruptive that the regular classroom teacher is unable to maintain order at a high enough level to keep the rest of the class from being negatively affected. The disruptive students have not acquired the skills nor the insights to interact appropriately in that environment. The time and energy required to teach the disruptive student those skills in that environment would mean that the attention of everyone in the class would have to be focused on assisting the disruptive student to learn more appropriate behaviors—to the detriment of all other goals for the rest of the class.

The school for healing requires a concentrated effort to assist behaviorally maladjusted students to acquire the necessary social skills to successfully interact with the mainstream culture in which they live. When the student has acquired the necessary skills, he or she can reenter the mainstream environment and be successful. This can be accomplished in a variety of ways. Partial involvement of the student in the normal school environment (with support systems in place) with gradual increases in exposure to the normal environment until the student is able to function fully is one strategy. Full immersion without gradual integration is another approach. The skills and needs of the student are the determining factor in the exact strategies to be used. In turn, the school for healing can serve as an intermediate point from a more restrictive environment, such as a psychiatric institution or a prison, before the young person returns to the regular school environment. Ideally, the needs of the student determine the transitional role that the school for healing plays.

It is important to remember that *the final goal for all of the students connected with the school for healing is full integration into the mainstream culture* for the personal benefit of the student and the collective benefit of the society. An adult is either contributing to today's culture or taking away from it. A contributing person helps society by enriching it with what he creates, by paying taxes for the collective services provided to society, and by providing support to those in his immediate environment. However, if an adult functions as an outcast and if he is not following the core rules of the culture, then the society has to cope with the results of his negative impact. Resources are expended to assist both the individual and the victims, to investigate criminal activities, to prosecute and incarcerate, to assist children of the individual because of his lack of responsible behavior, and on and on. One is hard pressed to find a situation in today's society in which the effects of an individual's actions are totally neutral upon the culture. Even people who try to remove themselves from the culture cannot stop impacting it. For example, a homeless person living on the streets of a city, trying to evade all authority, impacts the culture. Such simple issues as where he goes to the bathroom, where he sleeps, who he has sex with, how he gets his food, where he puts his trash, what his personal health is, and his vulnerability to catching a communicable disease all have an immediate impact on the culture. To not intervene by assisting our at-risk youth will have long-term, negative consequences on society. All of society suffers when a young person grows into an angry, hostile adult who has dysfunctional problem-solving strategies when interacting with others.

The specifics of the make-up of the school for healing will certainly vary from school to school. However, several basic components are necessary. These components include a small ratio of students to adults, a strong counseling program, a student-responsive creative arts component, a heavy focus on the positive reinforcement of cooperative behavior, and a structure that promotes student involvement in the maintaining of the school environment.

The school needs to be as self-contained as possible. It is providing a concentrated focus on teaching the students new social behaviors. A separate and safe environment in which at-risk students can experience transitional behaviors is far superior to an environment that mixes the public school population with the alternative learning population. Expected confrontations during the student's transitional phase are far too disruptive to the regular school program for both programs to exist under one roof.

Since the typical school for healing is in a self-contained setting, it needs to be large enough to benefit from the pooling of resources but not so large that all of the staff is unable to effectively learn about and respond to each student as an individual. When interviewed, the students were quick to say that having teachers take a personal interest in them was a new experience. Sixty students per school or school unit is a manageable number. For discussion purposes, we will use this size for explaining the basic internal structure of the school for healing.

The typical school has four classrooms of fifteen students each. Each classroom has a staff of one certified teacher, one teacher assistant, and one counselor. The individual classroom is loosely oriented around the concept of the one-room school. The fifteen students remain in a room with their designated teacher most of the time. Available on site are support personnel as follows: a full-time artist in residence; a full-time teacher having a specialty area in math, science, or reading who is not assigned to a specific classroom; a full-time professional who is the coordinator/facilitator between the school and other agencies, including the regular school programs; a school principal or director; a paraprofessional with counseling skills who can be present in a quiet and calming room; and a paraprofessional who provides specialized one-on-one assistance to students in such areas as computer usage, special learning strategies, and special projects. The school also needs secretarial and janitorial services. Additional support services from the school system and the community are required. All of these specialists and support personnel are focused to strengthen the one-room-school concept.

Generally, the students entering the school for healing are significantly behind in their academic work. Many have failed at least one grade and several subjects. Some may have specific learning disabilities, but the majority of the students' poor academic performances can be traced to a lack of basic skills in reading and math combined with very low self-concepts about their ability to do well academically. Naturally, these students have little motivation to try to learn. *In their minds, they know they will fail before they start.* Their records of achievement in school are not indicative of their intellectual capabilities; the correlation between their academic failures and their intellectual capabilities is poor. Experience taught us that once the young people encounter success at the school for healing, about ten percent or more of them will score at least 130 on individual intelligence tests.

The academic instruction for each student is built around the courses to which they are assigned in the regular school environment, tailored to their current academic ability. *The goal of both the student and the alternative school is to enable the student to accrue as much academic credit as possible toward earning a high school diploma from a regular high school program.* An individualized education plan is worked out for each student. *The teacher knows the academic and counseling goals for each student* in all of the activities the student encounters throughout the day. Individualized instruction does not mean the student works in isolation all day. *Group learning activities are encouraged.* Regardless of his or her reading level, each student can participate in a discussion on a history topic as it relates to the current culture. It is the teacher's responsibility, with support from the rest of the staff, to find ways of capturing the students' interests enough to induce them to participate. Because of the range in ages and the poor motivation of the students, teachers must be very creative in order to engage them in the learning process. The history and geography games introduced to the students while she was an artist in residence at CAL are good examples of the kinds of creativity necessary for effective learning among this student population.

Each of the four classroom teachers at CAL has developed a personal style of teaching that has been successful. While the school for healing has a common concept of education for the students, it also recognizes the uniqueness that each teacher creates for his or her own classroom. One teacher may function best in a classroom environment that utilizes drill activities more than others do. Another classroom may have its learning activities focused around student projects and dramatizations. School staff have greater flexibility to meet the individual needs and accommodate the individual learning styles of students when the administration takes full advantage of the special skills and creative energy of each teacher. Thus, *the student's learning-style needs are matched to the teacher's teaching style.* As a consequence of this sort of matching, each classroom is filled with students of differing ages and grade levels.

The counseling program is also geared to the individual needs of each student. The pairing of a specific counselor with a specific teacher is a collective process. The personalities of the two need to match as do their personal styles of interacting with the students. For example, a counselor who prefers to work with students in groups would probably be matched with a teacher who likes to organize a lot of special projects for his or her class. Both the teacher and the counselor must agree to being paired together, and they are paired before assignment is made.

The counseling program has two central themes. One is that *the counselor views each student as a very special person with unique talents and abilities* that the world needs. The second theme is an understanding that *from the student's perspective, he or she is always right in how he or she interprets situations and in how he or she reacts to them.* The fact that the student may be misinterpreting the situation or implementing corrective strategies that are counterproductive does not mean that the student is bad. It does mean that the student is making a mistake. This is an important frame of reference. Making a mistake is different from being a bad person. All of us make mistakes, and we can correct them.

An attempt is made to have each student in at least one group and one individual counseling session per week. The reality is that most of the students will be in several formal and informal group and individual counseling sessions. Sometimes the group session will be conducted by a different counselor than in the individual counseling session. The individual needs of the student, the expertise of a particular counselor in various issues, the social climate in the core classroom, and a host of other reasons will make this flexible approach to matching students with specific counselors an effective strategy.

One of the more interesting observations about this targeted population is that these students are so often artistically talented. More than one fourth of them have remarkable talents that would identify them as gifted people. Rarely are the students aware of their talent and rarer still is there a notation in their school records of any recognition of their talent. It is important that the school for healing have a component that fosters artistic expression. We are recommending an artist-in-residence program format; however, other effective delivery models exist.

Artists in residence enable students to see real artists producing real art for which they get paid. It also gives them the opportunity to see creative work at many stages of production. Artists rarely consider a project complete the first time they produce a piece of work. They refine and rework again and again until the piece feels right. This is a good model for students to observe, both in terms of their academic work and their life work.

Additionally, artists in residence can be liaisons for the school with the larger community of artists in the local area. Artists typically respond very positively to requests for volunteer demonstrations of their art; frequently they are willing to provide assistance for school art projects. Many of them remember their own frustrations with pubic school and can relate very easily to students at a school for healing.

The importance of the entire school being focused on the positive cannot be overemphasized. The students have a very negative view of school, learning, authority figures, and their own ability to be successful. They lack the motivation and interest to accomplish anything asked of them within the educational environment. The students simply do not think they can succeed; therefore, they do not try to succeed.

These students have become experts in being punished. Being punished is a means of gaining attention. Mainstream culture has focused on using punishment as its chief means of motivating children who are having difficulties. These students have a long history of being punished for being unsuccessful. They have been sent to the principal's office, suspended, lectured to, yelled at, and ridiculed so often that they have come to expect this as standard behavior from authority figures.

More and more punishment with increasing intensity has not worked and will not work to change their behavior. What will work is to *teach them to change how they feel about themselves.* Someone with a lot of patience must teach them that they have positive behaviors and characteristics. The students are worthwhile human beings; they can be successful. They have to learn this about themselves because it is outside their immediate experience. The quickest way for them to learn this is for someone to point it out to them over and over and over again until they really believe it.

We recommend the initiation of a positive behavior modification program into the daily programming of the school for healing. Numerous strategies have been developed that use behavior modification principles. Which one a particular school selects is a matter of staff preference as long as the program is true to the core principles associated with positive behavioral change research.

Without question, very demanding requirements are placed upon the staff of the school for healing. Teachers must continually use highly focused skills in this stress-producing environment. The school must have a continuing training program and a continuing emotional support program. *If the staff lacks the skills needed to work with these students, the program will not change the lives of the students.* Having a staff with the necessary skills will not make the school a success. The staff has to also be emotionally healthy. This will not occur by chance. *A clear strategy for maintaining the emotional health of the staff must be in place.* This important issue is discussed at length in Chapter 14.

CHAPTER 13

Philosophical Orientation

Recognizing and formalizing the philosophical position of the school for healing is critical to its success. Any organization or group has a philosophical position that unites it. Usually that position is not articulated. It is a generalized assumption that people loosely share. The set of assumptions the members have is more a product of their joint subcultural experiences than a carefully thought-out set of principles. Upon close examination of the belief systems of the participants in an organization, considerable variance in the details of what they believe will be found. An even greater variance exists between what a particular individual states as a belief system and how that individual behaves.

These individual differences magnify themselves in the group setting when the individual, group, or organization is under stress. The less the group or individuals in the group try to accomplish, the easier it is to maintain harmony within it. *When the organization makes a serious effort to bring about major change, it will encounter stress.* That stress will bring forth the underlying disunity of the participants.

The goal of the school for healing is to produce major changes in the behavior of the students in its care. The attempt to bring about such a monumental change in well-established behavioral patterns will produce significant stress in the school. Naturally the students who are the focus of the school's efforts are going to be under stress as they will resist adopting the new behaviors. The school's staff will be under stress because their attempts to change the students' behaviors are being resisted. The school system and the community will be under stress because they want results quickly and at a low cost, knowing that they are getting neither.

All of the players in this drama share one common belief. They all believe that they know what is right. They all believe that if the other participants shared their views, all would be well. None of the participants acknowledge that they may be wrong or that they are inconsistent in their own behavioral mandates for others. The only way to correct these deficiencies is to systematically set out to do so.

To state beliefs and then analyze behaviors initiates the process of bringing about consistency between what the individuals in an organization believe and how they actually behave. The behavior of the individuals in an organization reflects both the collective beliefs of the organization and the willingness of the individuals within it to comply with those beliefs. The articulated belief systems, or philosophies, of the individual or group are intellectual exercises. *The behaviors are an actual manifestation of an internalized belief system.* If the behaviors do not match the stated beliefs, then the stated belief systems are not the true beliefs of the individuals or group. *One can either change the behaviors to match the beliefs or change the beliefs to match the behaviors.* While the solution is easily stated, it is extremely difficult to implement.

The difficulties in implementing a strategy to promote greater consistency between stated belief systems and behavior can be underestimated. One of the biggest blocking factors is fear. *When fear is paired with habit, resistance to change becomes even more formidable.* Add to this the fact that everyone is pretty sure that he or she is right and that anyone who disagrees has to be wrong, and the difficulty of promoting significant change becomes clear. This scenario sets the stage for the justification of the use of force to impose one's will over the will of others.

The attempt to force one's own will over another's will has a well-documented history over the time of man's existence. It has also been demonstrated that lasting change does not come about as a result of this use of force. While it does force some people to change their overt behaviors, it does not change their belief system. As soon as the subjugated people can, they exert their will quickly, changing their behaviors to fit their long-held beliefs. As has been amply demonstrated by the world's numerous religious, ethnic, and political wars, hundreds of years of oppression do not change belief systems. The ancient Mayan and Aztec religions were not eliminated in the native populations by the Spanish priests. They were simply not openly practiced until the oppression against them was significantly reduced in modern times.

Imposing one's will on another does not usually change that person's belief system. As it is the belief system that ultimately controls individual behavior, it would seem obvious that our efforts to change others' behaviors must focus on changing their beliefs about themselves and others. This is certainly the case with adolescents who are having significant behavioral conflicts with others. It can be argued that the example of world conflict is not of the same nature as that of adolescents in conflict with authority figures. However, the basic principle is applicable to both groups. How a student's belief system directs his behavior in the classroom follows.

When one adolescent was asked why he was expelled from the public school program, he provided this explanation. He said that the very first day of school the teacher had it in for him. Right away she asked him where his textbook was. He told her that no one had given him one. She told him that everyone had been given textbooks in homeroom at the start of the day. She then proceeded to tell the class how important it was to bring the textbook every day and to complete the homework assignments if they were to do well in the course. The teacher never gave him a chance to explain that the school bus had been late, causing him to miss the homeroom period.

Next, the teacher assigned homework. The student reasoned that since the teacher had everyone's school records from last year, she had to know that the student had failed last year's course in that subject. He believed that the teacher purposefully assigned work that he did not know how to do. That night he did not do the homework because he did not know how to do it. He believed that the teacher disliked him and wanted him to fail. The next day in class, the first thing the teacher did was to ask to see his homework. When he told her that he did not have it, she asked him where his textbook was. He still did not have one. Once again, the teacher lectured the class about bringing textbooks to class and doing the homework. Almost every day this scenario played itself out until the student began cutting the class. His absences, which the teacher reported to the central office, got him into more trouble.

After he turned in a homework assignment, the final insult occurred. One day she made an assignment that he thought he could do. It was to find the answers to ten problems. That night he set out to work on them. The student and a younger sibling got into a big fight because the sibling would not turn down the TV; he could not concentrate. His mother's boyfriend broke up the fight, blaming the student for the trouble. This made him so mad that he did not sleep much that night.

When he turned in his homework at the beginning of class, the teacher said something to the effect that a miracle had happened—the student had finally done some work. When the whole class laughed, he was embarrassed. After the homework was collected, selected students were sent to the blackboard to show how they had solved the problems. While they were doing that, the teacher quickly graded the papers. Usually the homework is graded and passed back by the time the problems are worked out on the board. When he got his homework back, he had an F on it. She had checked off five problems as being answered incorrectly. Looking at the blackboard, he saw that two of the answers she had scored as wrong were in fact correct. That was the last straw. He jumped to his feet. With the paper held out in front of him, he ran to the teacher, yelling at her that she was a no-good blank blank blank who had cheated him of points. Because he stood up for his rights, he was kicked out of school. None of this would have happened if the teacher had been fair to him, he reasoned. He was a victim of the injustice of the system.

Attempting to argue specific points with a student or anyone else who holds a strong belief that is different from our own is almost always unproductive. Any attempt to suggest that an example given by the student might be wrong simply produces more examples of unjust behaviors of the teacher. Since he or she is convinced that the teacher was out to get him, the student can come up with endless examples of unjust behaviors. Any behavior the teacher displays has been and will be interpreted as negative by the student because that is how he or she interprets all of the teacher's behaviors. Punishing the student by suspending him or her from school does nothing to change his or her beliefs about the teacher. Logically, it can be deduced that the student will become even more angry, believing that the system unjustly supports the teacher. It is a small step from viewing the system as unjustly supporting the teacher to thinking that the system is also out to get him. Instead of teaching the student a positive lesson, the system has taught the student that it, too, is unjust. This idea puts the student into an even more rebellious mood. If the system's response is punishment, then the results will be counterproductive.

That the teacher in this case had a different interpretation of the situation is fairly certain. Whatever interpretation the teacher has of the situation, one thing is sure: The teacher interpreted her own behavior as reflecting only good intentions. One such interpretation could go something like this: She had reviewed the student's records and realized that he had failed the course last year. She also knew that the student was capable of learning the material but just did not seem to apply himself. She would motivate him to be successful in school. Noting that the student failed to bring his textbook the very first day, she decided to make a point to him as well as to the other students in the classroom. She deliberately selected an easy first homework assignment, but the student failed to turn in even a blank piece of paper. No textbook was evident day after day. Making it her mission to help the student, she continued each day to remind him that he needed to do better. Some days she just did not want to bring it up, but if she was ever going to be able to help him learn, she had to keep at it. She reasoned that, after all, if teachers give up on children, who will be there to help them? Then he started skipping class. She became worried that he would drop out of school. No matter how busy or tired she was, she made it a point to report his absences from class. Reporting him was the least she could do to try to keep him in school. Then one day he sprang out of his seat and rushed at her, holding the only homework he had ever done, unfortunately F work at that, and shouted obscenities at her. This was verbal assault. This was the thanks she got after all the energy she had put into this student. She concluded that teaching is hard and thankless work.

Everyone in this scenario is right. Each person views his or her motivations as just and good. Each person believes that the problems began when the other participant misunderstood actions and motivations. The student's interpretation of the teacher's actions make perfect sense, as he believed that the teacher had hostile and derogatory feelings toward him. Neither the teacher nor the student would disagree about the facts of what happened. The difference in the belief systems of the student and the teacher—the meanings attached to the facts—caused the conflict. Had the teacher realized that the student did not understand at all that she was trying to motivate him because she saw his potential, she could have tried to reach him in a more constructive manner. And had the student known that the teacher really valued him, he could have communicated his frustrations to her in a more constructive manner.

Experience tells us that much of intense conflict between school personnel and students is the result of a test of wills rather than the result of the student's misbehavior. The teacher, administrator, or school system employee is not going to stand for whatever it is that the student did in anger. The student is convinced that he or she is right and refuses to yield. The situation continues to escalate, with both parties exercising bad decision-making strategies. The student loses and suffers the consequences.

It is understandable that the student will make bad decisions—the student is an unformed adult. He or she is still in the process of learning social skills. On the other hand, the school system employee is a trained professional. The professional has no need to get into a power struggle with a student. When this happens, the consequences to the professional would logically be more severe than to the student. The reverse is more often the case. Because the student challenges an authority figure, the student is punished. The issue of whether the challenge was justified or not often becomes a nonissue. From the student's perspective, the system is unjust and the anger at the injustice is right. Sometimes, the student is able to agree that the way he or she expressed anger or tried to correct the situation was the wrong strategy. More often than not, though, that admission is a long time in coming.

Not too long ago a school administrator was observed giving an adolescent student a strong, verbal rebuke for wearing a hat while he was doing his schoolwork within a classroom. The teacher was also rebuked later for allowing the student to wear the hat in school. No written rules existed to forbid the wearing of a hat in a classroom. The teacher was new to the school, as was the student. Neither of them realized that their new educational community considered the wearing of a hat in the classroom to be a major violation of correct behavior.

The administrator felt that wearing a hat in the classroom was a sign of disrespect to the teacher. Since the teacher did not think it was a sign of disrespect (as evidenced by her lack of concern whether the student wore a hat or not), the teacher did not know what proper behavior was, reasoned the administrator.

If the student had been one who felt that his rights were being trampled upon, he might have argued his point. He could state that he was doing his assigned work and doing it well, so what difference did it make if he had his hat on? He could talk about seeing women wear their hats in buildings at school without rebuke. Pressing his point even further, he could argue that men and women in some cultures wear head coverings in religious buildings to show respect. The student could have been receiving chemotherapy and experiencing total hair loss, for which the culture found the wearing of a hat acceptable. For his final argument, he could restate that it made absolutely no difference in his ability to learn if he wore his hat; no one in the classroom had complained about it, so he was bothering no one. If anyone had a problem, it was the school administrator.

Aside from using bad judgment in continuously arguing his point and attacking the personality of the administrator, the student would have made sense. In fact, the student would have demonstrated that he had learned to think logically, putting isolated facts together to form a reasonable conclusion. Many educators would be proud of a student who had learned to do this. The school administrator reprimanded the student and the teacher because of social mores, not because of the hat's potential negative impact on the student's ability to do schoolwork. If the administrator had focused on social customs and the social message that is sent when a male student wears a hat indoors, the argument might have been avoided.

If both of them decided to make a stand on their principles, the argument would have escalated quickly. The student would not have yielded to the administrator's authoritarian proclamations. The administrator would not have allowed a smart-aleck teenager to defy her authority in the presence of a teacher and other students. The student would have been suspended again and again until his angry behavior left the administrator no other choice but to expel him from school. The student would lose; he never had a chance of winning a power struggle with a powerful adult.

Society would lose as well. The student would reach adulthood convinced that the system does not deliver justice, and he will probably refuse to live by the laws of society. He would be in trouble with the legal system and would lack the social skills necessary to employ his skills and talents. At a minimum, the citizens of his community would be denied his creative talents because his access to education was thwarted. At a maximum, community members would have to suffer the consequences of his antisocial behaviors and pay the costs of incarcerating him.

Unfortunately, relatively small infractions that escalate into severe penalties that are life changing is a reality for too many students. School systems, communities, states, and the federal government have set up rules that have mandatory consequences. These consequences can set up a chain of events that negatively change lives forever. Tennessee has recently passed a mandatory law that when a student drops out of school, his or her driver's license will be revoked. Many CAL students depended upon their driver's licenses for employment. This new law has the potential to create another downward spiral of events for CAL students. We must be aware of the consequences, especially for students living in poverty when such laws are made mandatory. Given the long-term consequences for students, society needs to rethink its policies regarding school policies and punishment practices.

At-risk adolescents have either given up on the school system and society or are close to doing so. They feel that they are being unjustly treated and that nothing they can do will change the situation. They are both desperate and depressed. The social consequence of having an ever-increasing number of young adults who believe that they have no hope of being treated fairly by society is chilling.

Each student is at a unique place in his acquisition of social and academic skills. It is important for the student to learn the accepted behavioral patterns of the culture in which he lives. He must understand that he is not protected from the consequences of deviating from them even when one thinks that he is morally right. The philosophy of the school for healing addresses these issues in a way that values the positive personhood of each student. Enabling the student to become an emotionally healthy and productive adult is the vision of each member of the team for healing. Constant improvements continue to be made in components of the school's delivery model as staff members become more skilled and experienced in implementation of various teaching strategies. This is expected and encouraged. *The anchor of the school is its philosophy.*

CHAPTER 14

The Emotional Well-Being of the Staff

The emotional health of the staff is vitally important to the success of the school for healing. The staff must respond to the inappropriate behaviors of the young people in an appropriate manner. The only way they can do that is to be emotionally healthy. When staff members function from a base of emotional security, they will react to unusual situations in a professional manner that reflects their training, their value system, and the philosophy of the school. At the time of interaction with a student, each staff person has to know and must be experiencing the reality that she or he is a worthy and competent human being.

To illustrate this point, place yourself in the role of a Sunday School teacher for three- to five-year-olds. It is time for the children to help you pick up the toys because church will be letting out shortly; the parents will be arriving to take the children home. You announce to the children that it is time to put the toys away. A four-year-old tells you that he does not want to stop playing. You smile and tell him that you are pleased that he is having a good time, but that it is now time to clean up. The child looks up at you and in an angry voice says that you are a SOB. Part of you wants to smile and part of you realizes that this child is telling you a lot about his background. You are saddened a little as you realize what this child's experiences must be like in other settings. Someone who has this child's respect has responded to frustration in exactly this manner more than once in the child's presence. At this stage in the child's life, he thinks this is the correct way to respond to frustration. You know better.

You do not feel that a four-year-old child can define your personality. You do not think that anyone would consider you to be a SOB because a four-year-old said that you were. You are not personally threatened, nor are you questioning your professional competencies on the basis of what this child has said to you. Because you are emotionally secure in who and what you are, you can respond to the child in a caring, professional manner that will enable you to help him to learn more appropriate ways to express frustration through both your spoken words to him and through the example you give him through your nonverbal communications.

Now change the example and insert a fifteen-year-old student into the scenario. You have directed the class to put away the textbooks to get ready to go to lunch. The fifteen-year-old says that he does not want to. You tell him that you are pleased that he is so involved in his schoolwork but that the class has to go to lunch now. The young person calls you a SOB. An emotionally vulnerable person will immediately feel threatened. She may shout back, "How dare you speak to me like that!" The student will, of course, shout back that he will speak to you any damn way he wants. The teacher will probably scream back that she will just see about that. The exchange becomes more and more heated, and the student is ultimately suspended from school.

As a result of the teacher feeling insecure emotionally and responding from a feeling of having her authority threatened, the situation escalated with the student losing in a big way. Who would prevail in a power struggle between the two was never a real question. The teacher has the entire educational and cultural establishment behind her. The young person has only himself. The reason the power struggle took place is that the teacher felt vulnerable. She was emotionally off balance at the moment of confrontation. The student's response to her provoked feelings of fear that if this student defies her and gets away with it, the other students will think they can do so as well. She will lose control of the class. If she loses control of the class, the principal will fire her. How will she and her children live? Such thoughts race through her mind. Thus, the student's opposition to her becomes an immediate threat to her survival and to that of her family.

From this perception of the situation, the teacher's overreaction becomes understandable, but it is still extremely detrimental to the student. The damage to the student goes beyond the immediate situation. As an authority figure, the teacher is a role model to the student. The teacher is teaching the student how to respond to confrontation. Her lesson to the student is that raw power and the imposition of one's will over another is the way to prevail in a conflict. If the student wants his will to prevail when he is in disagreement with someone, his strategy of choice is to use greater power or force. This is not an appropriate way of behaving for individuals, groups, or countries.

If our teacher of the fifteen-year-old had been emotionally healthy at the time of the confrontation, she would have responded in a calm and professional manner to the student's inappropriate behavior. A wide range of strategies could have been used to reduce the tension of the moment, turning the situation into a positive learning experience for the student. This is an important point. When the professional is responding from a sense of fear, the range of options is very limited. The opposite is true when the staff person is responding from an emotionally secure state of being.

One course of action the teacher might have chosen was to state how pleased she was that the student found some academic work so engaging. She could have suggested that he bring the textbook with him to lunch so that the two of them could discuss it together. She could also have expressed regret that he needed to express his wish to continue studying in so hostile a manner. She might have offered to meet with him and his counselor to find better, more appropriate ways of expressing his frustration. She might also have questioned her own listening skills to see if she had ignored earlier statements made by this student concerning his studies.

The point is that a four-year-old who calls you a SOB is not defining who and what you are. The four-year-old is revealing a great deal about himself and his past experiences to you when he curses you. As an adult, you are secure enough in your definition of the kind of person you are that a small child cannot threaten your own self-concept by his inappropriate behavior. It makes no difference if the person cursing you is four years old, fifteen years old, or fifty years old. It makes a difference only if you give that person the power to define you. This is not to say that you do not reflect on negative feedback to discover better ways of communicating or of accomplishing your goals. It is all right to make mistakes. All of us are engaged in a learning process. No matter what you know, many concepts are yet to be learned. Unless you have been trained to fly an airplane, you cannot do it. This has nothing to do with your personhood. It simply reflects your life experiences up to this point.

We know that our emotional states change. No matter how well we know intellectually that we need to be emotionally healthy all of the time, there are times when we are not. The reasons for being emotionally off balance are varied and may include an argument with a spouse at breakfast, a conflict with a child at home, the need to get to the bank immediately after school, or a sense of having more to do than you can get done. The point is that at times we all encounter things that emotionally upset us. None of us has reached that state of emotional health in which we are always well balanced. Rather than deny this fact of life, pretending that we are emotionally in control all of the time when working with at-risk students, we need to acknowledge and prepare for emotional stress. The consequences to the young people we are helping are too great to do anything less.

Each person on the staff of the school for healing needs to be able to remove himself or herself from contact with the students if they feel emotionally off balance. *To state that one needs to be away from students for that morning, afternoon, or entire day makes it so.* To allow this to happen means that school staff members make adjustments in their routines to accommodate the individual requesting a break. If the person is a classroom teacher, then the counselor and teacher assistant can manage the classroom for the designated time. The staff person needing time away from students could be the school's receptionist/secretary. Someone else (teacher assistant, principal, specialty teacher, volunteer) can fill that role. The entire school will make adjustments to allow someone who is emotionally off balance to be free of contact with students. To do otherwise creates negative consequences for students and the staff. During the course of the school year, every staff person will make use of this strategy several times.

The end result is that the students are almost always interacting with emotionally healthy adults. The sound professional judgment of adults serves as a daily model to the students of the ways in which successful people respond to stressful situations. The fact that each of the students at the school is so deficient in such skills means that they are constantly making mistakes in their interpersonal relationships with other students and with the staff. Their behaviors create moment-to-moment minicrises that could become major incidents any time that the staff is unable to manage them in a healing manner.

The high number of small but irritating incidents of inappropriate behaviors the students manifest throughout the school day can trigger an unhealthy emotional response in the adults so quickly that they may be unaware that they are caught up in the emotions of the moment. To plan for such occurrences rather than to deny that they occur is a sound policy. *Any time a staff member feels that another staff member has become emotionally involved in an interaction with a student, the observing staff member will immediately intervene by using a code phrase,* such as "Allow me to help" or "Can I be of assistance?" The coded statement lets the staff person currently interacting with the student know that the newly arrived adult perceives undue stress in the adult. The observing staff person will take on the immediate responsibility of the interaction so that the stressed staff person can withdraw both physically and emotionally from the immediate situation. At the moment the signal is given to withdraw by another, the staff person yields to the one giving the coded question. Conflict over this judgment call is rare. When a teacher, teacher assistant, or administrator begins to raise his or her voice in a discussion with a student, this strategy is implemented by the observing staff member. The agitated adult quickly recognizes during the first moments of withdrawal that his or her voice was raised, that breathing is at a rapid level and the blood pressure is up. Until they have time to reflect, staff members can become emotionally involved so quickly that they are unaware of engaging in inappropriate behavior with a student. *Staff members must prepare for such episodes by using strategies such as the one described above.*

Selecting the most emotionally healthy staff available is a step in the right direction. However, everyone on staff is considered to be in a continual process of becoming. Each person is expected to be more balanced and centered now than they were five years ago, and they are expected to be better adjusted five years hence than they are now. Selecting staff on the basis of emotional health is difficult at best. The difficulty stems from the discrepancy between what an individual has intellectualized about how to live his or her life and the actual behaviors he or she displays in stressful situations. Professionals can articulate the highest ideals about patience, understanding, and compassion for young people and still display hostile behaviors when a young person does not follow directions. Mocking students, making disparaging comments to them, pushing them, slapping a student, and so forth results in damage to that student's emotional growth. Working with troubled youth on the front lines of education is not the place for professionals with large disparities between their stated beliefs and their overt behaviors.

The discrepancies between what some new staff members say they believe and the ways in which they actually interact with troubled young people can be partially attributed to a desperate desire to be kind, understanding, and gentle—even as the new employee realizes that his or her behavior is quite the opposite. The discrepancies threaten their entire sense of who and what they are. Even when numerous staff members observe their inappropriate behaviors, some are compelled to deny that they did any of it because their concepts of personhood are so threatened.

Since experience teaches that a small but significant portion of new staff members are prone to display the above-described discrepancies, a probationary period of employment for all staff members is recommended. This probationary period can include several days of observing specific staff members model the school's philosophies, moving gradually toward the new staff member's direct control of a classroom or activity. A mentor can be assigned to advise and consult with the new staff person. The new person needs constant feedback on his or her responses to the students. In the event that the person is found to be unsuited for the full implementation of the school's delivery system, it is in the best interest of all involved to let the person know as soon as possible. It should be emphasized that the person needs to be honored for the intellectual level of understanding they have reached in knowing what needs to be done to assist the troubled youth. They have much to contribute. The individual probably already realizes that he or she is not suited for the particular stresses and challenges presented at this time by troubled youth. He or she probably feel relief at being released from the emotional stress they have been experiencing in the setting of a school for healing.

Unfortunately, the pressure to fill a staff position, limited resources in the school, and a host of other issues often create a situation in which the school needs a new staff person within a short time. These pressures prompt shortcuts that lead to greater risks of failure. Failure can result in one or more young persons being dealt with inappropriately, which prompts explosive and hostile behaviors in the young person. *When it comes to the emotional stability of the young people, only small margins of error are permissible in this setting.*

Let us revisit a scenario already described earlier, this from the perspective of the administrator. A loud shouting match erupts in the school hallway. The school administrator is in a nearby room. Immediately, he walks into the hallway to find a large male student shouting at a teacher while moving his arms in an agitated manner and pointing his finger at a female classmate. The teacher is shouting back. The classmate is also shouting as she stands slightly behind the teacher. Other students are pouring out of the classroom, forming a circle around the shouters.

Approaching the shouters, the administrator steps between the teacher and the male student. Standing 6' 2" tall, the African American fifteen-year-old student weighs about 220 pounds with no observable body fat. The petite teacher weighs approximately 110 pounds. As the administrator steps between the two individuals, he speaks to the young man in a concerned but soft voice stating that some terrible injustice must have just happened to him. The student turns to the administrator and shouts that he has been accused of stealing just because he is a black male. The administrator responds that discrimination of any kind is not tolerated at this school. He asks the student to tell him more about the incident.

In a calm, quiet, professional manner, the teacher has now focused her attention on getting the other students back into the classroom. She immediately stopped interacting with the student when the administrator spoke to him. This was the signal that she needed to let someone else defuse the situation because she was too deeply involved in the emotions of the event. The fact that a coded phrase was not used reflected both the crisis of the moment and a clear understanding and trust between the teacher and the administrator. The momentary interruption enabled her to refocus and collect herself so she could calm the growing agitation of the other students.

The fact that the intervening staff person happened to be an administrator was just a chance occurrence. At the school for healing, all staff personnel, regardless of job title, have the responsibility and necessary skill to intervene in similar situations. By choosing words that reflect a valuing of the student's personhood as well as a sense of justice, the staff member is able to temporarily ignore the inappropriateness of the student's emotional state while at the same time defusing it.

Calmly, and with concern in his expression, the administrator invited the student to an office so that the student could fully explain his sense of the injustice he had experienced. As they entered the office, the student was still speaking very rapidly and agitatedly; but he had stopped shouting. He told the administrator of his experience of arriving at school so hungry that he had a headache. He had requested the time-out room in order to cope. When he returned to the classroom, the first thing that happened was that a white female student asked him if he had seen her purse. He felt that he was being accused of stealing the purse because of his race. That was so unfair and that is why he lost his temper, he reported.

The administrator agreed that the situation seemed to be unfair. He asked the student if it would be all right if he, the director, went to the classroom teacher to make sure that she understood how unjustly he had been treated. The student agreed. After the teacher heard the student's story, she informed the director that the girl only asked the boy if he had seen her purse because she had misplaced it. He was the last person that she had asked because he was not in the room earlier. Upon being called over, the female student emphasized that she knew the boy had not taken it, but was only hoping that he had seen it when he was in the classroom earlier that morning. The director noted that the boy owed both the female student and the teacher an apology and asked them each if an apology would resolve the tension. Both the teacher and the student agreed to this.

The director went back to the angry male student and explained the beginning of the incident to him. The young man spontaneously said that he owed both the teacher and his peer an apology. He hoped that the administrator would allow him to do so before he was kicked out of school. The director reassured the student that he was not going to be expelled. He was informed that his anger was understandable as he had interpreted the situation; he had simply made a mistake in his perception. He had also made a mistake in the strategy he chose to correct what he thought was unjust treatment. The important points were that no one had gotten hurt, that he learned that he needed to get more information about situations before he formed his conclusions, and that he needed help in developing better strategies for correcting injustices. His counselor and teacher would continue to help him acquire these skills. Overall, the director concluded that the incident had been an excellent learning experience for the student. This was the mission of the school.

In order to give this young man the opportunity to apologize, both the teacher and then the female student were brought to the school office. The young man apologized most graciously and the two accepted the apology in like manner. He returned to the classroom for an incident-free remainder of the day. Sessions with his counselor would be arranged to help him develop better strategies for dealing with similar frustrations.

If the teacher had responded to this student from an emotionally off-balance position, the student could easily have ended up in jail. For example, she could have demanded that he get out of her room and go to the principal's office. If he refused by violently shouting and calling out insults to her, she could have pushed him toward the office. He could have pulled back and pushed her. Given his great strength and the depth of his anger, he could have pushed her hard enough to knock her down, constituting teacher assault. Further complicating the issue is the high probability that other students in the class would have intervened to try to protect the teacher. A major fight could have erupted. The strength of the male student and his high degree of agitation at this point would make it almost certain that bones would have been broken or other serious injuries inflicted.

None of these events occurred because the teacher was emotionally stable throughout the incident, although she did become emotionally off balance enough to begin to shout. Fortunately, the school had anticipated such types of stressful situations and had a working strategy in place. *The incident ended up being a minor one from which all involved persons learned something.* The classroom was able to return to normal.

CHAPTER 15

Management Strategies

M aintenance of the staff's emotional health is a continuous process. Enabling the staff to have a degree of control over the decision-making process is a key component in the process. To that end, the administrative management style is oriented toward the participatory management approach. In essence, the teachers and staff members collectively make the policies of the school. Naturally some policies are imposed by state law, school system policies and procedures, and so forth that the school must follow. Despite these limitations, a considerable number of decisions can be made by the group.

Some of the decisions left to the staff are the specific rules of the school, special events, and the use of volunteers. Someone on the staff may have an idea for improving the control of movement of students in the school. Using the participatory management process, the person would present the idea at the weekly staff meeting. The proposal would be discussed and voted upon. If it were adopted, the entire staff would be responsible for implementing it. The behavior of the school administrator is an important factor in this process. The administrator must support the opinion of the majority, even if he or she disagrees with the decision. The disagreement of the school administrator will have been voiced during the discussion phase of the process. If the arguments of disagreement did not persuade the majority, then the decision to implement the strategy must be supported by the administrator.

The typical administrative style in U.S. schools might be called a benign dictatorship. The school principal practicing this style is usually a pleasant person who uses well-developed communication skills to talk with teachers, central office staff members, and the general public. This type of principal fosters the formation of teacher committees that make recommendations to him or her. The principal then decides if he or she will implement them. He or she usually explains to the teacher committee why he or she is not going to follow their suggestions. When the principal sees something happening that he or she does not like, he or she immediately decides what needs to be done and then directs the staff in how to do it.

For example, in an alternative school setting, a principal may decide that when the students move from classrooms to a nonclassroom activity, such as going to lunch, the students do not have enough adult supervision. This could lead to noisy hallways, rowdy behavior, graffiti written on the hall walls, and so forth. In the opinion of the administrator, the situation needs correction immediately. She decides that the classroom teacher assistants need to be reassigned from the classrooms to hallway monitoring during the transition periods. One morning she posts a list of new assignments for the teacher assistants. Each assistant is assigned to a specific location in the hallways fifteen minutes before and after every student transition period. The teachers and assistants are to implement the plan immediately.

The problem with this management strategy is that it undermines the emotional security of the staff and the students. Since the emotional stability of staff members is a significant factor in their ability to respond in a professional manner to the many inappropriate behaviors of at-risk students, it is important to maintain that stability. Several potentially negative consequences may arise from the principal's dictated changes. Individual teachers may need their teacher assistant in the classroom all of the time to accomplish specific lesson plans. Without the assistant there, the teacher will have to readjust the lesson plans that she has been developing for several weeks. Since the students have a problem adjusting to rapid changes in their environments, the change in the classroom could be the spark that triggers a major incident in the classroom. The mere fact of the teacher's fear that an incident is more likely now adds to the tension that threatens her emotional stability. The teacher assistants may feel that their opinions do not matter in how they are utilized. Feeling undervalued and dispensable, they may be more predisposed to respond in a negative manner when they encounter negative behavior in the hallway. Their response to students could be the triggering event to an incident.

When the principal makes a unilateral decision that affects the school, she is making an underlying assumption that she possesses all of the facts relevant to the entire situation necessary to reach the correct solution. Given the wide range of student problems and a large staff with diverse personalities and skill levels, it is unlikely that this is a correct assumption. If the principal's assumptions are wrong, the implications for the school become obvious. Even in the unlikely event that the principal's solution is the correct one, another erroneous assumption is made. She assumes that the staff will see the wisdom of her decision and willingly follow it. Under the circumstances, this assumption is simply wrong. When a school staff is ordered to implement a decision that they do not agree with, it is fairly certain that the solution will not work—even if the mechanics of the solution are implemented.

An administrator following the benign dictatorship model of management is probably pretty good at it. The fact that she has always used it and has risen to an administrative level in the school system indicates her ability to make correct decisions at least some of the time. However, when dealing with the intensified situation created in a school for healing, the shortcomings of this administrative style become magnified to the extent that they are counterproductive.

A commonly observed behavioral characteristic of the benign dictatorship style of management is a misinterpretation of the open door policy for staff to communicate with the administrator. Generally, the open door policy refers to the chief administrator's encouragement of subordinates at any level to schedule an appointment to discuss concerns the employee may have. On the surface, this is a sound policy that enables the administrator to gain information that could help the entire organization to function better. The misuse of this policy occurs when the administrator responds to the information. The personality that chooses the benign dictatorship administrative model likes to control situations and is good at it. The tendency for this personality is to take the information from one or two individuals presenting a problem and then to make a decision on how to correct it. A directive is given to the rest of the staff about new behaviors to use for an old problem.

This administrative behavior creates two key problems for the school for healing. First, the administrator has not heard all sides of the story. Since the problem involves people, the problems often revolve around someone not doing something right or someone doing something that creates a problem for someone else. Because she does not investigate all aspects of the problem, including another party's point of view, the administrator will make mistakes that detract from the effectiveness of the organization.

The second problem created when a principal responds unilaterally to problems is that divisions are created within the staff. Whoever talks to the administrator and gets results has gained a share of the administrator's real and perceived power. Factions are created within the school that compete for the ear of the administrator. Since the administrator's time is limited, she cannot spend all of her day listening to individual staff members. Unless problems are solved during staff meeting time, it would take undue time to keep all members informed and to give each staff member a voice. Factionalism among the staff is detrimental to the overall philosophy of the school and to the morale of the staff.

The obvious advantage of the benign dictatorship administrative style is that decisions can be made quickly. It is assumed that the administrator has good decision-making skills and is the most knowledgeable individual for making decisions. The logic supporting this administrative style is that the decisions the administrator makes are usually correct. Since U.S. culture has such a high incidence of benign dictatorships at all levels of its society, adults are most familiar with it and adjust to it fairly readily. When the staff becomes stressed, they will revert from other administrative styles to the dictatorship approach out of habit. Therefore, an argument can be made to do that with which everyone is comfortable. The flaw in that argument is that in the high stress environment of the school for healing, the margin for error is so small that mistakes will significantly reduce the school's effectiveness in assisting children.

This is not to say that the school will fail to assist all of the children. It will not. The simple fact that the troubled youth are getting more individualized attention than was the case in their last educational placement communicates to them that others see them as valuable. For some, this is enough assistance to make a difference.

The cultural stereotype of Clint Eastwood as a hard-nosed Marine sergeant provides a good illustration of the power of attention, even negative attention, upon the self-concept of young people. The sergeant is tougher, shouts louder, and demands more of the soldiers than any adult they have ever known. The sergeant is in the faces of the young soldiers, constantly yelling that they never do anything right. He also makes their lives miserable when they make mistakes. Since the sergeant is always there, the sergeant and the soldiers get to know each other well. The sergeant expends considerable energy to teach the soldiers what he knows. An emotional relationship is established between them. For troubled youth, this may be the first in-depth emotional relationship they have ever had. As the training progresses, the soldiers conform more and more to the wishes of the sergeant. Significant portions of society approve of the behavior of the soldiers because they do what the sergeant wants.

The proponents of this type of behavior modification strategy might recommend it for the entire nation. For obvious reasons, it is doubtful that the majority of the nation wants to be treated in this manner by employers, politicians, or educators. This is neither the most effective way for people to learn nor the most effective way to establish supportive relationships with others. However, the cultural myth exists that it is a good way to deal with people who do not want to learn or do what authority figures want them to do. This is true only as long as the proponents of the approach are the implementers and not the recipients.

This myth has fostered the creation of military-style boot camps for youth and prisoners in many parts of the country. Since the myth is so well established in this culture and the culture is under stress in relationship to coping with at-risk youth, the culture has a tendency to choose this strategy despite more effective options. The boot camps have no doubt helped some young people, but they have not produced the hoped-for results. I contend that if the same amount of money, energy, and resources were committed to implementing the delivery model offered by the school for healing, a far greater number of young people would be helped.

Participatory management approaches are the ones most often cited when referring to the more democratic administrative styles used within educational settings. Several variations of this management style exist that use many different terms to express similar concepts. One such term is site-based management. The recommended management style for the school for healing is the participatory management style explained earlier in this section.

The participatory management style engages all of the staff in the decision-making processes of the school. In addition to federal and state laws, the local school system also has rules and regulations that must be followed. Yet a large number of internal situations lend themselves to the group decision-making process within the school. *The overall structure for allowing the group to make decisions is the staff meeting and the committee framework.* When policy issues, rules, or activities need to be decided upon, anyone can bring them up at the staff meeting. The staff members make decisions about such issues at the meeting or create a committee to study all aspects of the issue and present recommendations to the full staff. *The majority rules on contested issues.*

Sometimes only certain sections of the staff need to consider specific issues. The guidance counselors may have a particular concern that affects only them, so they can elect to reach a consensus, informing the entire staff of their collective decision. *Every staff member must be aware of the counselors' strategies in order to support them.* Sometimes staff subgroups think that a matter affects only themselves and then discover that other subgroups are affected as well. *Any staff member can put an item on the agenda for consideration.* Enough advance notice of an agenda item must be given so that the full agenda can be printed and circulated to the entire staff to review before the meeting takes place.

The underlying principle is that *everyone has an important perspective on the operation of the school,* regardless of the job title. Each staff person is an expert at his or her job and can make special contributions to the functioning of the school. No one person can know what is best for all. No one person can implement any rule or policy of the school single-handedly. If the school for healing is to effectively implement its philosophy and methods of assisting students, the management of the school must be collectively done in a way that requires the active participation of all staff members.

The principal is a key factor in the success of this approach. If the principal agrees to this management style but overrules the staff on a decision that they make, then participatory management is not operating. The principal is really functioning under the benign dictatorship administrative model. Since the principal may actually have more experience than the rest of the staff in decision making, the principal may be correct in disagreeing with the staff. That disagreement needs to be voiced during the staff meeting. However, during the time of voting, the principal has only one vote, as do each of the other staff members. In turn, the principal is as responsible as the rest of the staff for implementing the collectively made decision.

Individual and collective commitment of all staff members to this management style is crucial. Staff members are also members of mainstream U.S. culture and are collectively more familiar with the benign dictatorship style of management. When some staff members encounter disagreement with a decision the staff made as a whole, a tendency arises to form small groups or factions that attempt to force their will on the entire school. This becomes more probable when the stress increases. Democratic processes are learned behaviors. In the reality of the workplace, some people never get the opportunity to learn the democratic way of making decisions. While it is clearly the culturally expected behavior for educators to speak highly of democracy, they are often not treated democratically. Thus, while a staff person may enthusiastically praise the democratic process as a way to manage a school, his or her behavior may sometimes be seen as an attempt to subvert the process. The principal's yielding to the group's decision is interpreted as a sign of weakness. A weak principal is interpreted to mean that a decision-making vacuum in the school must be replaced by strong leadership. Factionalism within the school has the potential to undermine the philosophical base under which it operates.

Correcting the emergence of factionalism within the school for healing is an important issue. It will almost certainly manifest itself because of the lack of training and personal experience most educators have in managing a school in a democratic manner. The temptation for the administrator is to arbitrarily remove the dissonant individuals from the school. Again, the benign dictatorship model is easily brought to the forefront by those under stress who have experienced that model more than any other.

The philosophies of the school as well as participatory management style must be followed with the staff and the students if a true school for healing is to exist. Specific strategies to use for all situations cannot be provided. Instead a wide range of strategies need to have been developed in anticipation of such situations. If they do not work, then others need to be applied. It is important to remember that the staff is in a process of acquiring skills. No staff person arrived at the school with all of the skills desired, including the principal. Everyone is becoming better. *Everyone is becoming more skilled in applying the principles of the school through what they say and what they do.*

A number of strategies might be used to work with staff members who wish to change the participatory management style to the benign dictatorship model. Conferences with the agitated individuals might help them resolve the discrepancies between their philosophical commitment to participatory management and their behavior that tries to bring about benign dictatorship. Management strategy meetings might be arranged between the stressed individuals and those with whom they are in disagreement to try to find common ground. An independent consultant could be brought in to hear the issues and express an opinion. The important point is to reduce as much stress for the individuals involved in the conflict as possible so that their reason rather than their emotions can prevail. When the participants are free of emotional stress, they can remember that they agree on the same philosophies and principles. They are just disagreeing about which are the best and most efficient strategies to use.

Factors beyond the school walls may cause major complications in efforts to resolve internal misunderstandings that arise as a participatory management style is introduced. The school system's central office staff may be opposed to the participatory management concept. This can happen in school systems and states that have philosophically embraced the concept. It is always the behavior under stress that exemplifies the true belief system. Central office staff members opposed to the participatory style will be prone to encourage staff from the school for healing to talk to them, using the open-door policy. The central office staff will tend to support the school building staff, who tell them of decisions made at the school level they did not like. Without getting any additional information, the central office staff will make a decision to change the school-level decision and order the school principal to implement the new decision. When the school principal tries to explain the reasons for the original decision, the central office staff indicates that they just don't have time to debate the issue because they are so busy. This approach is very destructive to the school. It is possible, but not likely, for the school to continue to follow its philosophies if enough of the staff have a strong commitment to them. The undermining of a participatory management decision by those in greater authority is much more destructive to the school for healing than is criticism of the school from other sources, such as the school board or the community. Misunderstandings from these sources can be overcome through effective communications and site visits.

On occasion, there may be a staff member who reaches the conclusion that he or she does not agree with the school's philosophies and principles. This does not mean that the staff member is a failure. It simply means that he or she has learned that he or she functions better in an educational environment other than that created by this type of school. This awareness needs to be honored by giving the individual assistance in finding another school or professional setting in which to make his or her contribution. Sometimes the staff may be aware that a particular individual's behavior toward them or the students is such that it is clear they do not believe in the school's basic philosophies—even though that individual says that they do. It then becomes the principal's responsibility, with the support of the staff, to help that person understand the situation. It may mean that a more suitable place of employment will need to be found for this individual, also. At some level, the individual in question knows that he or she is not happy or functioning appropriately. A better way of making contributions to society exists for that individual; he or she needs to find it.

Several levels of management decision making exist within the school for healing. In the classroom, three adults must make decisions together concerning the management of the classroom. Those decisions need to be made in the same manner as for the whole school. The teacher assistant does not have the expertise to tell the teacher that she needs to change from one strategy in teaching math to another. The assistant does have the expertise to note that one student spends more time on his schoolwork when circumstances are one way as opposed to another. The list could go on and include school volunteers, specialty instructors, and outside-agency service providers.

The most obvious drawback to the participatory management process is the time it takes to make decisions. There is never enough time to study every aspect of an issue; yet decisions must be made. Mistakes will take place. Anticipate them and be willing to make adjustments when they are discovered. If mistakes are not occurring, then the ability of the school to do better is thwarted. Every mistake is an opportunity to discover how to better serve the students. Since the student body is constantly changing, specific learning experiences for the young people need to be adjusted. Change and learning to do better are constants in life and must be seen as opportunities. Experience has taught us that the participatory management strategy provides the most productive framework for allowing the goals of the school to be successfully implemented.

CHAPTER 16

Positive Reinforcement

Negative instructional statements made to students, such as "That is the wrong answer, try again." "I told you yesterday how to do that; were you not listening?" "You need to pay more attention." "You did not do well on your homework on this part either." "Why do you not study harder?" "Where are your worksheets? The answers on them are probably wrong, too" are an attempt to motivate and teach. These negative statements are a common occurrence in the public education classroom. Sadly, the majority of educators still use more negative feedback than positive feedback in their interactions with students. It is encouraging to note that almost all educators articulate adherence to the belief that students are to be valued and to be told in a supportive manner that they are valued. Not integrating this belief into their behavior is a common cultural shortcoming.

The teacher skilled in positive reinforcement makes instructional statements to students in the following manner: " I liked your approach to this problem." "I can tell that you really tried to work this out." "You have been so patient in the face of this frustration." "This part of the solution shows me that you are thinking. Let us take advantage of it to see how we can find the correct solution." While acknowledging that an error has taken place, the praise is genuine. By the time an adolescent has failed several subjects, has had serious behavioral difficulties in school, and has had legal problems in the community, it is a fairly safe bet that the significant adults in the adolescent's life are focused upon his or her negative qualities. Teaching a troubled youth that she is a positive person who is valued and needed requires consistency and patience. Since what is being taught is true and was once believed by the student, the reteaching process takes a lot less time than it took to teach the student that he or she is bad and cannot succeed in mainstream culture.

Using a student's successes as a way of helping to improve reading levels demonstrates a sound strategy. The teacher takes a college textbook off the shelf and out of it randomly selects a paragraph. Explaining to the student that this is a college textbook, the teacher asks the student to read the paragraph as well as she can to see how many words she can read. After counting the total number of words in the passage, the teacher informs the student of the total. When the student begins to read the paragraph out loud, the teacher notes what words she gets right. Typically, the student reads simple words, such as "the" and "and," correctly but rushes through long words, such as "environment." The student's basic strategy is to sound out part of the word, hesitate, become frustrated, and quickly make up something so that she can move on to the next word. When the student finishes the paragraph, the teacher adds up the number of correct words and gives the student the total. It will be a small number. The teacher tells the student what percentage of the words she read correctly. Typically, the percentage falls around 10% to 15%. Then the teacher points out to the student that she has displayed some very good word-sounding skills that indicate she is a better reader than this score reflects. The student will probably not believe the teacher. The teacher then explains that on a specific word the student got the beginning sounds correct.

For demonstration purposes, I will continue to use the word "environment." The teacher points out that the student got the "en" sound. Since what the teacher says is the truth, the statement serves as a reinforcement to the student. Then the teacher states that she noted that the student became frustrated and made up the rest of the word, saying that it was "engaging." Pointing to the "v" in the word "environment," she asks the student what sound it makes. The student makes the correct sound; and the teacher says, "Yes, that is right," or some other reinforcing statement. The teacher helps the student discover that he knows the sound of the letters and can, with patience, sound out the word.

Context and clues are also used to assist the student in solving some words. Simply asking if the word makes sense in the sentence inspires the student to solve it. After going through all the difficult words in this manner and allowing the student to solve them, the teacher asks the student to reread the paragraph. The student will correctly read a significantly higher number of words than he did the first time. It is then pointed out that if the student is patient that he can read at a fairly high level. In the past the student has simply become frustrated with the process and quit too soon. The student has the skills to be a good reader but has simply not practiced them enough. The stage is set to continually support the student in reading practice. If the strategies are to have their maximum desired effect, the teacher needs to be positively reinforcing and encouraging.

The school must also establish behavioral goals that are within the student's reach. Students whose difficulties in the regular school environment center on frequent losses of temper will display frequent losses of temper when they first arrive at the school for healing. To tell such a student that he will be expelled the first time he loses control at the school means that the student will be expelled. When the student comes to the school for healing, the time for pretending is over. The staff cannot pretend that a warning will cause the student to change a behavior that is well ingrained.

The first task in allowing the student to gain control of her temper is to set a realistic goal for improving the control. If the student loses her temper once every hour, then the goal may be to control her temper for a 75-minute period. Naturally, the staff will help her develop strategies for doing this. One set of strategies may be for the student to signal the teacher when frustration begins so that the student is allowed to leave the learning task or the immediate social setting temporarily. When the student can keep control her temper for a 75-minute period, a new goal can be set for longer and longer periods of time until the student has achieved complete control.

For both academic and behavioral goals, Bailey and Morton's (1970) RAID approach, introduced in Chapter 11, is a well-organized method of positive reinforcement. *"R" stands for "rules" in the RAID strategy.* The student needs to know what the rules of conduct are for the school, the classroom, and for his unique situation. Having the rules clearly articulated enables the teacher to be consistent in reinforcing the desired student behavior. It is critical that the students participate in the creation of the classroom rules. They are creating their own environment and subculture. If students are going to follow the rules, they must have a personal investment in them.

Classroom rules must be stated positively. Typical rules include: "Everyone will be allowed to finish a thought when speaking." "The room will be clean at the end of each day." "Each person will be treated courteously." "The class schedule will be followed." "Students will be seated and ready for assignments at 8:30 a.m." "Individual study periods will be honored with quietness." "Staff directives will be honored."

Strategies that will assist in the rules process include keeping the list of rules short. Rules need to be written and posted in a conspicuous place. They need to be referred to often. Rules can always be changed: What was a good rule that addressed a problem two months ago may not currently be relevant. A rule may have become so automatically incorporated into the classroom culture that it is no longer needed as a guide to the conduct of the class. Different rules for different activities can exist. When a new student is assigned a classroom, a first process must be to orient the student to the rules.

Rules that address each student's special needs or problems also must be established. One student may have a rule that he will study without communicating with others for fifteen minutes at a time during classroom work time. Another student's special rule could be that he will speak without using curse words for five minutes at a time during classroom discussion. A third student's special rule could be that she will be in her seat ready to work three mornings a week at the start of school. Each of these student-specific rules reflects graduated steps in reaching more appropriate social or educational levels of functioning for every student.

The student-specific rules often exempt him or her from following general classroom rules but are designed to move the student into closer compliance with those rules. When students are not capable of following the broader rule, they are exempted during the learning process. The opportunity to acquire the necessary skills to follow the broader rule is provided. The other students are able to accept the exemptions because they know that people are unique and have special issues or needs through which they have to work. They have all experienced the need for such exceptions themselves—even if the exceptions were not available to them. The school for healing provides such opportunities.

Internalized self-approval independent of external reinforcement is the final goal of any approval process. Ideally, human beings are able to provide their own reinforcements. Few adults have reached this state of being. Young people are in the process of becoming; they need the approval of others to know if they are learning what the culture expects.

"A" stands for "approval" in the RAID strategy. The at-risk students have such a negative conception of their own talents and capabilities that subtle approval messages alone do not have the power to change behaviors. Positive reinforcements must be immediate and tangible. A token system is an immediate and reinforcing strategy to which students respond. It immediately demonstrates to them that they are being successful, that they are perceived as successful, and that they benefit from their successes. Again, the ultimate goal is to no longer need to use external reinforcements, such as a token system.

The simplest way to set up a token system is to create a monetary system. The school prints its own play money and uses it to reinforce appropriate behavior and academic progress. As those who have used this system with the at-risk population can attest, the play money becomes very valuable to the students in a short period of time. Measures must be taken to prevent counterfeiting and theft of the play money. Play money lends itself well to the teaching of banking principles through the establishment of checking accounts, interest payments, and the like. The students willingly elect bank officers and follow money-management decisions. The potential to use stock-market quotes to teach math concepts is readily apparent.

A key procedure in setting up the token economy system is providing items and activities for the students to purchase with their earned play money. Since adults do not always know what is valuable to the students, students must be engaged in this process. Few students would be willing to spend the play money it took them two weeks to earn in order to listen to a Mozart symphony for ten minutes.

A list stating how a student can earn points and what the current purchasing power is must be posted in each classroom. A typical list of ways to earn points might include the following:

1. Five points for being one of the first three students in one's seat ready to start work at a designated time,
2. Three points for completing an assignment,
3. Six points for getting an A on an assignment,
4. Two points for completing a designated classroom chore, and
5. One point for following teacher directions.

Points for accomplishing individual goals can be negotiated between teachers and students.

A list of purchasable items or privileges must also be posted. The restrictions on when the items can be purchased, used, or consumed must be written out so that misunderstandings can be avoided. A list of things that could be purchased might include the following:

1. Listening to a radio station on headphones for fifteen minutes (15 points),
2. Playing a board game for twenty minutes with a friend (25 points), or
3. Sitting with a student from a different classroom during lunch period (18 points).

The desire of the students for a particular activity, the amount of energy the staff has to invest in providing the privileges, and the amount of points the students have on hand or can earn all play a role in determining the number of points each privilege will cost.

When first implementing the token system, the teacher must be liberal in passing out points. The students will be unfamiliar with the system. When the students first come into the classroom and it is time for everyone to be seated, the teacher has a good opportunity to begin distributing points. The teacher can speak the names of each of the two students already seated, thanking them for being ready to begin work as he or she hands points to each of them. This gets the attention of several other students as they mill around. As the next student moves to his seat and sits down, that student can be rewarded with a point as well. In a short time, the entire class is seated; however, several students are still talking to each other. The teacher can then distribute additional points to those who are quiet and ready to begin while thanking them for following the classroom rules. The teacher's discretion determines whether everyone will ultimately receive a point for being in his or her seat and quiet during the initial stages of the program.

After the program has been in effect for a few days, the pattern is set for receiving and redeeming points. At that time, the teacher will move away from liberal distribution and toward awarding points according to the posted rules. The distribution of points and the thanking of students who are ready to begin the day as required is a pleasant way of getting the class settled and the day started. It is certainly superior to the stereotypical approach of trying to gain control of the moment by shouting at the class that they are too noisy and they had better get to their seats if they know what is good for them. The teacher has control of the distribution and redemption of the points. He or she can either inflate or deflate the amount that is distributed to students as the situation warrants.

The students have to want to earn the points if the system is to have an impact on their behavior. If they are not cashing them in, the ways they can spend them are probably not attractive to them. Giving students input into the ways points will be cashed in is the solution. The students in one classroom may want the opportunity to walk to a corner convenience store to purchase a snack item. It could be arranged so that a maximum of five students could go to the store with a staff person on Tuesday or Thursday afternoon from 1:30 to 2:00. It would cost each participating student X number of points per trip. After this privilege becomes more popular, the number of points needed to obtain the privilege could increase.

The point system serves several purposes. It gives the student immediate feedback that he or she is doing things right. It also serves as a reminder to the school staff to reward those who are following the rules and that the class can be managed by focusing on the positive behaviors of the individuals. The system also instills an immediate sense of accomplishment in the students. They know that they are being treated fairly and can have privileges because of their good work. This process serves as a triggering device that helps students change their views of themselves—instead of seeing themselves as failures, they are now able to see themselves as achievers. They will begin to perceive authority figures as their champions who are encouraging them on to success in contrast to their previous perception that authority figures were oppressive figures constantly trying to catch them disobeying the rules. Under this system, the teacher is placed in the position of encouraging a student to complete one more goal so that he or she will have enough points to purchase a highly desired privilege.

As the point system develops, its potential to assist students at several levels expands. One area of assistance it provides is in getting needed clothing to students who would not accept the same items as charity. The idea that poor adolescents living in welfare conditions want handouts is a myth. They have a great sense of personal pride and avoid charity items at considerable personal suffering. During the cold months, they would rather be cold than accept a coat as charity. Racks of coats that are desirable for both their stylishness and their quality will go unclaimed even though a student's need is great. When it is announced that the coats will be auctioned off for points, the picture changes. Students begin hoarding their points, making trades with other students to pool their points, and finding new ways to acquire them in order to make the highest bid for a desired coat. Once the coat is obtained, the student wears it with pride. This process also promotes cooperative behavior and the building of group interaction skills. Both of these characteristics are demonstrably lacking in at-risk students. They must be provided the opportunity to develop them. The point system promotes this learning process.

When a negative incident occurs between a staff person and a student, the staff person may feel tempted to punish the student by withholding or taking away points the student has earned. This must never happen. The student earned the points and has a right to use them at the designated time in the preestablished manner. Certainly the staff member would consider it totally unjust if the administrator approached him at the end of the month to say that because he did not like the staff member's performance in a certain situation $100 will be withheld from his paycheck. The staff member would state that he had earned the money and had a right to it. If the administrator wants to set parameters on future earnings, that would be another issue, but to take away already earned funds would not be right.

A consequence of inappropriate behavior is a failure to earn points. When the student wants to eat lunch with a friend but has not earned enough points to do so because he has failed to complete a school assignment before lunch, he is experiencing the consequence of his lack of motivation and productivity. Assuming that the assignment is within his level of accomplishment, his decision not to complete the task provides an immediate consequence that he does not like. His counselor can make various analogies to assist the student in understanding consequences. For example, when an employee does not show up for work on time, he may miss important instructions. For the at-risk student, the pattern of blaming someone else for the negative consequences of one's own behavior occurs frequently. The point system can assist the student in better understanding the causal relationship between his personal behavior and his failures or accomplishments.

Sometimes rule breaking benefits society; the rules could be wrong. Dr. Martin Luther King, Jr., made this point quite admirably. Yet, there were immediate and negative consequences for the civil rights protesters for not following the established rules. They were aware of those consequences and chose to suffer them for a better future. In working with the at-risk students, the school for healing was not trying to make them become social conformists. Rather, it was trying to help them become socially responsible citizens who understood the consequences of their behavior, who made informed decisions, and who had the necessary skills to attain the productive goals they desired.

As stated earlier, the ultimate goal of any behavior modification program is to move the student to a point at which he or she is intrinsically motivated. Members of the educational community, as well as members of the larger community, may criticize the point system for rewarding students for doing what they should be doing anyway. The counterargument to that is simple. The students were not behaving the way they should; past attempts to force them to do so had been unsuccessful. The point system is a tool to help the students logically and systematically acquire the behaviors that society wants them to have. As the point system enables the students to learn how to behave appropriately in various situations, a transfer occurs from using points as rewards to using praise and expressions of appreciation as motivators.

The counterargument to the point system is that the school is bribing students to behave. This is an interesting argument. If a person in this culture gets paid for doing a job, is that person being bribed? The person is being rewarded for work well done. If a student does excellent schoolwork and gets an A, we do not say that the student was bribed to study. The point system is a reward system that demonstrates to the student that he or she has been successful in accomplishing a behavior or task that was difficult. The student is being praised for an accomplishment with a token of value.

The "I" in RAID is for ignore. When the student displays inappropriate behaviors, the first corrective action taken through the RAID approach is to ignore it. As an example, if a teacher requires a student to raise his or her hand to answer a question, the teacher must choose to ignore the shouted-out answer and praise another student for raising his or her hand. By doing this, the teacher accomplishes two tasks. First, he or she reinforces the behavior of the student who raised his or her hand and followed the rule. Second, the teacher reminds the shouting student that the class rule is that students who wish to be recognized with the correct answer need only raise their hands. The vast majority of inappropriate classroom behavior can be handled in this manner.

For those relatively few incidents in which inappropriate behaviors must be corrected immediately, *the last component of the RAID system, "D" for disapproval,* is brought to bear. As with the reward system, several levels of disapproval must be considered. They range from a disapproving look to expulsion and incarceration. Disapproval is not the same as punishment, although many people try to make the two terms synonymous. In our culture, punishment is more closely linked with the concept of revenge. Within the school for healing, the concept of revenge or punishment has no place. There are consequences for inappropriate behaviors. If the student fails to complete a classroom assignment, he or she will not get a point. If the student comes to school with the smell of alcohol on his or her breath, the parents will be notified to pick up the student, and a conference date will be established to determine if the student should remain at the school. He or she might be placed in a rehabilitation program for more concentrated assistance. If the student begins to shout and be disruptive toward another student or staff person, that student will be immediately separated from the other party and consulted to determine the cause of the his or her anger. Specific strategies will be initiated to correct the situation and to cause the student to learn better coping skills for the future.

Sometimes student actions threaten the safety of themselves and the entire school population. If a student brings a weapon to school, the proper authorities will be contacted immediately; they will remove the student to police facilities or take other appropriate action. The staff will appear in court or before other authoritative bodies to speak of the student's positive behaviors and successes, but they will also testify that the student had a weapon in school. Consequences are in place for inappropriate behaviors. When those consequences are brought into play within the context of the school environment, they need to be carried out as soon after the display of inappropriate behavior as possible. Once the consequence is experienced, the incident is considered a matter of past history and need not be frequently reviewed.

Just as we all do, at-risk students make mistakes. But some of their mistakes can bring consequences that affect the rest of their lives. This does not mean that their lives are over. Although individuals who are incarcerated for committing a crime have a criminal record, many are able to become happy and productive citizens after they have served their time. The interventions and support of caring adults can help at-risk students channel their talents and desires in a positive direction. Almost all at-risk young people have the potential to have a bright future. The positive reinforcement system is an important first step for many of these students in learning to use their energies wisely and in ways that benefit society.

When the positive reinforcement system is implemented along with the other components of the school for healing, very few incidents of inappropriate behavior of consequence ever occur. The overall behavior of the students becomes so positive and polite that it is frequently difficult to convey to visiting officials the fact that the students do have behavioral difficulties and are the same students who were so hostile and disruptive in the normal school environment. As one would expect, without a positive reinforcement system, the school environment would be filled with hostile and disruptive incidents.

It should be emphasized that teachers and staff must be trained in this process. It is unrealistic to expect that the entire school staff will have the ability to be positive with students 80% of the time when staff persons first arrive for employment. Understanding the RAID system does not mean that they are able to implement the system in a classroom environment. The training of the teachers must reflect the principles of the RAID system. If the trainer cannot be positive with the teachers 80% of the time in helping them implement the system, then the trainer has demonstrated that the system cannot work.

Whenever children or adults are learning new things, they will make mistakes until they have mastered the task. There is nothing wrong with making mistakes, nor is anyone considered to be inferior because he or she is in a learning process. Making a mistake indicates that the person is trying to do better. It is the trainer's (or educator's) responsibility to present to the student new goals that are within the student's capacity to achieve. If the teacher is able to be positive with the students 40% of the time when he or she is first employed, the immediate goal for him or her may be to increase positive comments to a 50% level and so on until the 80% level is reached.

Videotaping the teacher's interaction with the students or directly observing teacher/student interactions are two good training strategies. An independent rater will evaluate the positive and negative responses to students. In the early stages, the evaluation process has the potential to be devastating to the teacher. The teacher knows the philosophy and views himself or herself as a highly competent professional who has incorporated the values of the school into his or her belief system and life. Since the teacher has never before had the opportunity of being observed and evaluated on how positive and consistent he or she is with students, the teacher has never had objective feedback as to how his or her behavior fits the desired pattern. When the teacher hears how far short of the goal of 80% positive reinforcement his or her behavior falls, he or she may feel temporarily demoralized. The trainer must be prepared to point out the positive things that the teacher does and how easy it will be to build on them.

A relatively simple observation strategy for the trainer to use is as follows. Write at the top of a sheet of paper a title for classroom rules; then skip a few lines to write down a heading for implied rules. Moving down a few more lines, divide the paper into two columns. At the top of the left column put a plus sign and at the top of the right column put a minus sign. Just before the observation takes place, note what the formal rules of behavior are for the classroom. If they are not posted in the classroom, the teacher will probably state them for the activity that is about to begin. An example would be the teacher telling the students to clear their desks because it is now time to begin a discussion. The rule is that the desks are cleared during class discussions.

After the formal classroom rules are jotted down, the actual observation can begin. It is helpful to note the time the observation begins and ends. The teacher thanks a student for clearing his or her desk, and a mark is made in the plus column. In contrast, when the teacher tells a student that he needs to clear his desk, a mark is put in the minus column. After the second student cleared his desk, the teacher smiled at him and a mark was put in the plus column. During the discussion, the teacher tells a student that she is speaking too loudly. This is an implied rule that "students need to speak quietly during discussion." The implied rule needs to be written under the space made available for noting implied rules on the evaluation sheet. In this case, a mark also needs to be placed in the minus column.

In about twenty minutes of using this observation technique, a fairly good understanding of the reinforcement style and consistency of the teacher can be gained. Through sheer force of will, those teachers not skilled in the positive reinforcement model may be able to be 80% positive for the first few minutes of the observation. However, after about five minutes, the intense focus necessary to manage a class of at-risk students removes any pretense of behaving in any other manner than the teacher's natural pattern.

If the teacher falls short of having 80% positives or lacks consistency in following rules, care must be taken on the observer's part when reviewing the observations with the teacher. The goal is to help the teacher improve from where he or she is now to reach the ideal state; the trainer must maintain sight of this goal. All of the staff members are in a process of becoming better, just as the students are. If staff members cannot implement the overriding philosophies of the school, they can hardly expect the students to do so.

Staff members are teachers not only to the students but to themselves as well. If staff members find that they are unable to implement the school's philosophy in their daily interactions, then the philosophy of the school must change. The components of the school's philosophy should be so sound that each person's implementation of one of them serves as a demonstration of its positive impact on others. The school for healing is a very pleasant place to be. Visitors like to come because it feels good to be there among all the caring staff and students.

CHAPTER 17

Networking With Other Agencies

The relationship of the school for healing with the rest of the school system is critical. It is important for getting the students who will benefit from the delivery model to the school for healing; it is important for returning the students to the regular school environment. Many of the students who have been attending the school for healing can return to the regular school environment in a relatively short period of time (three months to a year) if they are provided a support system at the regular school. *In a spirit of genuine cooperation, the school for healing and the referring school need to exchange information and strategies to assist the students in transition.* It is possible for some students to return to their original schools and be successful without the cooperative support of the staffs, but it is more difficult. Without the support, the student tends to remain at the school for healing longer until he or she has fully mastered the necessary skills. The longer stay is a waste of valuable resources because a waiting list of students in crisis usually exists.

Another reason to have a good relationship with the rest of the school system is the support that the school system gives to the school when it comes under criticism from elements within the community. Too often a negative incident becomes the focus of public attention. *No matter how many students the school helps, there will be those who feel that its basic strategy is wrong.* This most often comes in the form of stating that the students are bad people who should be punished rather than given special assistance. The critics would prefer the alternative school to have been such a negative, jail-like experience that students, upon returning to their referring school, will want to be good so that they never have to go back to the horrible alternative school. The fact that the students are often reluctant to go back to the regular school environment is proof to the critics that the students are being rewarded for being bad when they should, instead, be punished. If there are professionals within the school system who also hold these views, they can undermine the successes to such a degree that the concept of the school is abandoned.

One would think that the parents of the students who have achieved success would strongly support the school to the general public, but that is usually not the case. In most cases, the parents are embarrassed that their children ever got into trouble and do not want to be openly associated with that trouble or with the school. Notable exceptions to this reality exist, but they are few. Some parents feel guilty about some of their parenting skills and do not want others to scrutinize them. A few of the parenting adults have done less than admirable things to their children and do not want anyone to know about it. Most of the parents are caring individuals who are frustrated and perplexed about the behavior of their children. Once parents realize that staff members want to help their children rather than punish them, parents become responsive to suggestions and advice from the staff. The vast majority of parents have very full lives with little time to do much more than what they are already doing. It is difficult for these parents to come to school meetings to learn and implement new strategies for relating to their children.

Other human service agencies of the community are important counseling and support components of the school for healing. Logic tells us that if a student is having significant behavioral difficulties in school, he is also having the same difficulties outside the school environment. He is probably having relationship difficulties in the community, in the family environment, and among friends. If the school's work is to have a lasting, positive effect upon the student, extenuating circumstances within the at-risk student's environment must be addressed. *The collective problems of the at-risk student population are often so massive that no one agency has the resources or authority to address them appropriately and independently.*

In most communities, the school system is the largest agency that serves children. It has the highest number of counselors, social workers, truancy officers, nurses, and trained psychological workers. However, school system administrators typically know very little about what other government and community agencies that serve children can do for them, such as to place them in foster care or in group homes or to provide them with financial assistance from social services. The school system is seldom involved in juvenile justice or probation hearings and refers very few students to social services for such issues as malnutrition, child abuse, or chronic medical problems. In turn, few agencies advise the school system that they are involved with the children because of these problems. One notable exception is a growing cooperation between law enforcement agencies and the schools. In more and more communities, the probation officer is becoming an important part of the school system's planning team for troubled students.

It is highly probable that every student at the school for healing is receiving services from one or more human service agencies outside of the school system. The fact that a student may be appearing before a review panel to determine if he or she will be placed with a different set of foster parents tomorrow will have an impact on the student's emotional state during the current school day. The school staff needs to be aware of this and make special arrangements to minimize stress-inducing situations for the student. The probation officer needs to know of a breakthrough one of his parolees has made at school to avoid a temper outburst so that he can develop supportive strategies through his offices as well. Students can benefit in many ways from the exchange of information and coordination of efforts between school staff and representatives of child-serving community agencies.

Staff members who work with at-risk students quickly become aware of the benefit of such interactions and become the strongest supporters of coordination activities. The obstacles to this cooperation are most often individual agency rules and regulations, different philosophies about how to treat at-risk students, competition for limited funds from a common funding source, or misplaced agency loyalty. Sometimes professionals mistakenly pair their own identity and competency with the agency for which they work. Consider the experiences of a group of newly graduated doctoral-level psychologists who are seeking employment. They all apply to five or six agencies near the university. A few months after they become employed by various employers, each of them begins claiming that their agency is the best and that the others are not as good. The mental health center provides better therapy than the school system does. The school system assesses children with emotional problems better than the hospital does. The sexual assault crisis center provides better therapy than the mental health center does. As they try to foster employee loyalty, the agencies often promote these comparisons.

The truth is that they are all employed to serve the public, not to serve a specific agency. The funds provided to school systems, the juvenile justice system, and human services agencies are funds designated to assist children with problems, not to build agency empires. Something is wrong when a school superintendent is forced to deny funds to a school like the school for healing while he has a waiting list of those who need and want to attend a school that even he or she acknowledges is turning students' lives around. The superintendent is aware that for each student who is helped, society saves about a million dollars in incarceration expenses and other social services. Lost tax revenues from the work the student might have had as an adult must also be considered. The probable life of the young person who is not helped includes being in and out of trouble and in and out of jail. His children will probably have difficulties that require social services. Also to be considered is the cost to his probable victims.

The superintendent notes that society does not give him a million dollars for each child who is turned around by the school for healing. Yet the public provides funds to help troubled youth. They want and need their money to make a difference. They are not concerned about which agency does it. They are aware that no one agency can do it all. They expect cooperation among the various agencies and professionals who assist the young people. It must be remembered that the agencies and the professionals are a reflection of the culture in which they exist. The problems that they have in cooperating are problems of the culture and of the people who live in the culture. We are all part of the problem. Part of the solution rests in each of us.

Local colleges and universities are good sources of volunteers and resources, as is the community at large. The school for healing needs these individuals. The volunteers can provide specialized instruction (research, math, art, and so forth) and mentoring. They can serve as excellent role models for the students. *The volunteers must be screened and monitored carefully as they interact with the students.* Once the volunteer pool is tapped, the chief difficulty will be in how to integrate them into the program's activities. The time it takes is time well spent.

CAL received enormous help from the local university. First, the athletic department released well-known basketball and football players to implement athletic games at the school for healing. Not only did the athletes plan the activities, they competed with the CAL students, becoming friends and role models for the students. This gave classroom teachers planning periods during the week that they would otherwise not have had.

The college of education at the local university assigned their students in educational counseling programs as interns to our school. As the university student was always paired with a professional counselor, the placement was excellent training for entering the "real world." The liaison provided opportunities for social interaction between the high school student and the college student. Achievement goals and objectives could be discussed one on one.

The law school at the local university had a program in which they presented ways to promote conflict resolution and street law. Their program encouraged role play of different forms of conflict as well as step-by-step procedures for dealing with the parties involved. This program was an asset in showing our students that conflict can be dealt with through communication rather than through fistfights and gang wars.

In addition to our visiting artist program, individuals with special talents also volunteered. One university professor came in to teach about writing for the local newspapers. The CAL students wrote some articles about the school that were published locally. During the process, the CAL students complained that the professor never had a good word to say about their work. He was always critical. The professor was proud of the work the students had written and did not perceive that there was any problem. We worked it out. Our students depended upon being told first what they did right before they were told how they could improve their work. Once the professor learned how his method of teaching made the students feel inferior, he quickly changed his method, noting the strengths of writing before proceeding with his critical analysis.

Engaging volunteers is a good way to keep the community informed about the true nature of the school for healing. The community at large and the immediate local community in which the school is located have reason to be concerned about the activities of the school. They realize there is a concentration of young people with problems at the school. They fear that the school will promote more problems. These fears need to be acknowledged and addressed. When a nearby house is robbed, it is reasonable for the victims to wonder if the robbers might have come from the school for healing. Only by being informed of the programs and activities of the school will the community understand the nature of the program and its value to them. The volunteers are good sources of information about the school to the community. They can counter rumors and calm the effects of rhetoric from those who do not support the philosophies of the school. Once the majority of the community understands the school's program, support is usually widespread.

Our students decided to produce a small school yearbook. A computer business located nearby offered space in their classes for CAL teachers to come and practice page layout as well as basic computer skills so that they could pass their knowledge on to the CAL students. The students sold advertising to local businesses, with great success. A printing business in town worked diligently with us in order to produce a yearbook of which everyone could be proud. The computer business charged us nothing; the printing business charged us at their cost.

One of the many problems of at-risk students is their sense of alienation from any community. By engaging volunteers and businesses from the community at large, the young people start to become connected to members of the community in a positive manner. They begin to develop a sense of belonging that they may have never had before. It is this connectedness with citizens outside of their immediate and limited circle of acquaintances that enables them to develop a feeling of commitment and responsibility for promoting the general good of the culture.

The programming of the school for healing stresses conscious efforts to build a sense of belonging in the classroom and in the school. As the student becomes a contributing part of the school, steps are taken to promote the same connectedness with the community. The strategies used by the school to these ends are numerous. Assigning each student a job in the school is an obvious strategy to help him become a contributing member of the group. Some jobs enable the student to earn points for completing them while the more popular jobs require the student to pay points for the privilege of doing them. Typical school jobs include sweeping the floors, taking out the trash, cleaning the blackboards, straightening desks, making photocopies of handouts, managing the class bank for the points system, setting up the public address system for the fashion show to be held by the school, decorating the classroom, removing graffiti from the building, weeding in the school garden, publishing the school newsletter, and more.

The students at CAL are actively engaged in planning special events and in carrying out the activities to prepare for events. Numerous opportunities arise for students to speak to groups of other students about their successes in creating the special events. In order to accomplish some of the more complicated jobs successfully, the students must engage the support of others. This process teaches the students the value of working together and builds a sense of commitment to those who help them promote their activities.

The community offers opportunities for field trips to symphony performances, a Christmas ballet, storyteller performances, and museums. At first, the community is reluctant to allow the "bad kids" to attend. Our good reputation within the larger community stemmed from the high level of trust the staff members had that students would conduct themselves properly. This is not to say that there were never problems. On rare occasions, a student was quietly removed from a performance and taken back to the school. When this happened, the student lost the privilege of attending such events until he or she was able to demonstrate the acquisition of better social skills required of one in a large public setting. *Adults cannot teach students how to behave appropriately in public by keeping them inside the classroom;* students learn through experience. Peer pressure from those at school arising from their own embarrassment about another student's inappropriate behavior and the dire consequences of such behavior is likely to provide the most effective training for the incoming student.

One university professor who was conducting a research project at the school created a volleyball team at CAL. Regular practice sessions were held; teamwork rather than individual success was emphasized. The team became skilled enough to compete in the regular school league, sometimes winning the game. The professor was surprised at the good sportsmanship demonstrated by the CAL students during scheduled games. The students loved to compete; students who misbehaved were temporarily denied the privilege of the opportunity to play against other teams. Of course the CAL students made every effort to practice good sportsmanship on the team so this highly valued privilege would continue to be granted.

Once a student has experienced this process, they commonly return to their home school and volunteer to be active participants in such activities as the school newspaper, the peer mediation program, or the street law seminars. They join community groups, making significant contributions to them. Most of the at-risk young people have always wanted to belong to the community. They simply did not know how to do it and had not acquired the social skills necessary to be effective participants. Added to their difficulties was their sense of rejection and isolation from the community. The school for healing has simply provided them with the opportunity and the necessary skills to be that which they have always wished to be: valued and positive contributors to their culture.

CONCLUSION

We were pleasantly surprised to see how quickly many of the young people responded to the environment we created. There were remarkable positive changes in their behavior. We saw angry, hostile individuals become gifted public speakers. Young people who could only express anger to authority figures became peacemakers. Students who always failed became successful scholars. Parents and adolescents were reporting better home situations.

After admission to the school, it took about two weeks for a student to begin changing from being hostile and confrontational to the CAL staff to being a more pleasant and responsive person. The students had expected to be treated the same way they were treated in the regular public school program. It took a lot of self-discipline on the part of CAL's staff to avoid reacting to the hostility of the young person and to continue demonstrating to the student that the staff saw many positive attributes within him. After a couple of weeks of this treatment, the student's behavior changed from that of hostility to one of respect and then to one of caring for the staff and their fellow students. The change was so remarkable that we had difficulty convincing visitors that the students had had such a bad record of behavior in the public school setting.

We had public school supervisors come to the school for the purpose of renewing their own emotional energies. They would just sit in classrooms without directly interacting with the students or staff. They stated that the pleasantness and courtesies of the students and staff with each other was reaffirming and gave them a sense of peace in knowing that schools could really be positive places for everyone. The sense of mutual emotional valuing and support between students and staff was so strong that when a student returned to the regular school setting, he or she often came back to CAL during afterschool hours to do volunteer work and to tell of his or her successes in other environments. It was as if the young people were coming back to tell an older relative of their successes, knowing that the relative would be as proud of the successes as they were. Of course, the

young people were right. The CAL staff was very proud of the
accomplishments of its students wherever and whenever they occurred.

Not all of the students made the remarkable changes that others
accomplished. It became clear to us that some students needed to remain in
the emotionally supportive environment created by the school for healing
for extended periods of time. They could make social and academic
progress in this environment but could not do so in the public school
setting. Other students had such severe problems that CAL could not assist
them enough. These few individuals needed much more than CAL had to
give. Those young people who were heavily addicted to drugs or alcohol or
had suffered brain damage from such substance use fell into this group.
Others could not control their angry impulses in almost any social
situation. A few young people who came to CAL were unable to respond to
any adult direction. Their presence was simply too disruptive to the school
environment. The staff would spend almost all of their time managing the
continuous crises in which these individuals were involved—to the
detriment of all the other students.

Another pleasant surprise was the discovery that so many of the
students were artistically talented. We would not have made this discovery
had it not been for Rosa Kennedy's involvement with the students and her
engagement of the region's artist community to work with the students.
Almost all of the students who came to CAL had never had art education in
the public schools. They were as surprised to discover their talent as the
CAL staff was in finding it. Visitors to the school often asked to buy
student art work that was on display.

In many cases, the discovery of artistic talent gave the young people an
enhanced sense of self-worth that provided a significant boost to their
ability to learn academically. There were times when a student's ability to
understand a math concept or another academic concept was clearly
enhanced. We never fully understood why it was so, but it happened.

It became clear to us that if more public schools would embrace the
strategies that we used at CAL, the large number of students being
suspended and expelled could be significantly reduced. At that time, the
area's public schools' records indicated that one out of every four seventh
through twelfth grader was suspended at least once during the school year.
Within that group of students were individuals who had been suspended
multiple times. Even if the public schools adopted CAL's strategies and
obtained the same positive results, it was also clear that there were students
in the public schools who were so badly damaged behaviorally that they
could not function effectively in that environment. In addition, the public

school could not efficiently serve the other students with these students present. In today's society, there is a need for a school for healing, such as CAL, regardless of the effectiveness of the public school environment. In turn, some young people need a more intense helping environment than can be provided by a school such as CAL.

It is sad to realize that many troubled youth exist in our culture. However, it is reassuring to know that we can really help them. The major blocking variable is the lack of public will to provide that help.

One of our most frustrating experiences in gaining support from the public schools for the model was the refusal of a few principals to believe that any of the students had changed in general or that the specific students they knew had changed at all, regardless of the presented evidence that verified the positive changes. This meant that when a specific student returned to such a school, the school administration seemed to focus on trying to catch the student being "bad" while ignoring the student's positive behaviors. Such an environment made it harder for that student to continue being successful. Remarkably, many did so. It was encouraging to find that many principals were supportive of the school for healing and of the young people when they returned to their public schools.

The belief we held that the young people in trouble are caring individuals who are more positive than negative was confirmed by our experiences. They see themselves as heroic figures surrounded by personal and social injustices. Arguing with them about a specific situation in which their behavior was "wrong" is fruitless. Even if the adult "proves" his specific point, the young person can and does bring up other situations in which they were unfairly treated, thereby making a legitimate justification for their inappropriate behavior. The adult cannot prevail in situation-specific discussions with the troubled adolescent concerning the youth's inappropriate behavior. The use of authoritarian power over the student to force compliance when verbal discussion has failed to convince the young person of his errors simply reinforces his belief that the system is unjust.

From the adult's perspective, there is no question that the student in trouble is making an error in the behavior he displays. The adult is interpreting the behavior with a different understanding of the meaning of the facts surrounding the situation. The adult is also interpreting the situation from a different range of experiences to draw upon for comparison purposes. It is clear to the adult that the young person's behaviors will have negative consequences for him and for others if those behaviors are allowed to continue.

Controversy among educators and other members of society begins with the selection of strategies to use in changing the student's behavior. By the time the student's behavior was considered so bad that he was sent to the school for healing, he had experienced a long series of attempts by administrators to force him to be "good" through the use of punishments. Many of the punishing strategies were revengeful. The underlying lesson that seemed to be taught to the student was that those with power prevail over those who do not have power: If you want your will to prevail over another's, then you must have power. The rightness of your position or your ability to communicate effectively with someone plays little or no part in whether your position prevails. Most mainstream school officials would argue that this is neither what they believe nor what they teach. However, when the discrepancies between what they say they believe and what their behavior indicates they believe are analyzed, one often reaches the conclusion that they believe that the use of force is the best way to bring about behavioral changes in troublesome students. This belief seems to be strongest when the officials think the student is challenging their authority.

Many school officials make the mistake of considering punishment to be synonymous with negative consequences; in reality, the two are quite different. If a child is careless with a chain saw, the negative consequence may be that he cuts off his hand, a consequence that he will live with the rest of his life. It does not mean that the child was an evil person who must be punished so that he will be careful with a chain saw in the future. It was clear to us that punishment is not a good teacher and that encouragement for doing better was our best teaching strategy. There were enough real sociological consequences to our students for displays of inappropriate behavior that our task was not to find additional ways to punish them but to find ways of giving them hope that they could change their lives for the better.

This is not to imply that there was a lack of consequence for inappropriate behaviors at CAL. The most obvious consequence was the lack of a reward. More intrusive consequences were logically attached to behaviors that warranted it. For example, if a student brought a drug to the school, the staff would immediately notify the proper authorities and the child's parenting adults—as it is required to do by law. In turn, the staff would also tell the juvenile judge or others about the positive things the same student had done at the school. The point is that consequences to inappropriate behaviors exist, and CAL upheld them; but CAL did not invoke additional punishments for those behaviors, nor did it seek revenge against the student for the poor behavioral choices. Every culture has its set of rules for social behavior that it expects its members to follow. Whether those rules are just or unjust, consequences occur when they are not followed. We do a disservice to the young people to teach them otherwise. Of course, if a rule is unjust, the student needs to know how to change it. CAL taught that as well. It engaged the students in creating the school rules and in modifying them when that was also needed.

The school for healing saw its role as teaching students how to interpret social situations in a different way than they had in the past and as teaching students more effective strategies to change real social injustices that they encountered. The staff worked hard to avoid engaging a student in an argument over the facts of a situation. Instead, they concentrated on helping the student understand how their antagonists could interpret the same set of facts in a way that enabled them to view themselves as just and noble people with the student being the bad person. Once the student could do this, they could either understand a mistake they were making in their interpretation of the situation; or they could discover new strategies for more positively interacting with the individuals. This approach was effective with many of the young people, but it did not work with all of them. Some of them were so badly damaged by the quantity of negative things that had happened to them that CAL did not have the resources to work with them as intensely as was needed.

We learned that our core assumptions about how to assist the students to become more successful with their lives were correct. In the process of trying to implement those assumptions, we learned a great deal. For example, we learned that

1. A lot of truly bad things have happened and are happening outside of the school environment to the young people who are being suspended and expelled from school. Our human services support system is not able to assist many of these children, or the children do not have access to the system when it can assist them.

2. The emotional well-being of the student is first and foremost. At times, the academic learning of the student has to be put on hold until the emotional well-being of the student is established.

3. Teachers need to value the positive qualities in each student. In order to do this, they have to be both emotionally healthy and utilize their highest forms of professionalism.

4. The emotional well-being of the staff is critical to the success of the school. The staff does its most important teaching through their spontaneous responses to unplanned events. They are often the only emotionally healthy role models the students have a chance to observe. How staff members respond to the many unplanned and potentially stress-

inducing events of the day serves as immediate teaching models for the students to draw upon when they are in similar situations.

5.   An emotionally healthy school staff does not occur by accident. There must be a proactive administrative design within the school that promotes and maintains the emotional health of the staff. This includes providing the staff with a degree of control over their work environment, allowing them to remove themselves from contact with students when they are feeling emotional distress for whatever reason, and having quiet time for themselves during the school day.

6.   Participatory management was found to be an effective model for the school. It drew upon the staff's combined knowledge, allowed for the creative responsiveness necessary to meet the needs of the students, and promoted the emotional well-being of the staff by giving them control over their work environment.

7.   The one-room-school concept appears to be the most functional model for these students, with specialty teachers coming into the room to supplement the regular classroom teacher's academic instruction. These troubled young people need a stable classroom environment that takes on the role similar to that of an extended family.

8.   Students need to be taught academics at their actual level of expertise rather than at any arbitrary grade level attained. The appropriate level for each subject needs to be determined either by testing or by curriculum-based assessment.

9.   The students need to become active members of the school community. However, when the student came to CAL, he or she had not learned how to be a positive participant in the community. CAL had to be very active in getting them involved in group participation for the common good, a skill they lacked, yet needed to acquire. Once it was gained, the students did not want to relinquish it. They used it in the public schools and remained in communication with the CAL community.

10.   A team of three, consisting of a certified teacher, a teacher assistant, and a licensed counselor, needs to be in a classroom of not more than fifteen students, directing the studies of each student. The student goals must be the development of social skills as well as academic learning. Changing the composition of the classroom to serve more students, to have fewer staff members, or to have a staff that is less qualified will significantly reduce the effectiveness of the program—which can quickly become a very expensive baby-sitting program that produces no change of consequence.

11.   Counselors need to be accessible to the students by being in their

classroom and interacting with them on a daily basis and interacting with them in a variety of ways.

12. Teachers and counselors are expected to attend planning meetings with each student and his or her parent(s) or caring adult(s) to plan the student's immediate learning goals, whether academic or social. Of course this time must be provided to them to attend the meetings as part of their job description.

13. Each teaching team has its own style, and each style needs to be honored and valued. This allows each classroom to have a distinct personality to which the personality and learning style of the student is matched.

14. The students need immediate reinforcement for any improvements in their current levels of functioning. Teachers, counselors, and teacher assistants all need to be actively involved in a concerted reward system. The school for healing effectively utilized a token economy in which points were used to demonstrate to the student an immediate success toward attaining the student's stated goals. The RAID behavior modification model was implemented by CAL. This model allowed the teaching team to become cheerleaders for student personal growth.

15. Critical incidents within the classroom are perceived to be learning opportunities during the process of student change. Strategies for positive social interaction are analyzed, developed, and practiced.

16. The time-out room is an extremely important component of the school. A student could ask to go to the time-out room in order to remove himself or herself from a stressful situation, or a staff person could ask the student to remove himself or herself to the time-out room. The student had to have an academic assignment with him but was not required to work on it. The time-out room was for reflection and cooling down. There was always a staff person in the time-out room. The student could choose to engage in a discussion with the staff person, listen to soothing music, sleep, and so forth as long as he or she did not interrupt the activities of others there.

17. An art program is an integral part of the alternative learning process. Students can experience a way of expressing themselves without having to use verbal communication

18. Community volunteers are important components of a school for healing. These volunteers give a lot of positive attention to these needy students. This can be accomplished by simply practicing listening skills, tutoring, or just being a good friend.

19. Community support was critical to the existence of CAL. In

general, the community-at-large is afraid of troubled youth and angry at their behavior. The cultural response is to want to make the lives of the students as difficult as possible. The community has to be continuously informed of the mission of the school, its activities, and its successes if it is to survive and continue assisting young people.

20.   The professional staff is the link between the student and outside services. These services might include group homes, detoxification centers, juvenile court systems, drug rehabilitation programs, twenty-four hour mental health services, or child protection agencies. A high percentage of the students at CAL were having to draw upon community assistance services. As mentioned before, a lot of bad things are happening to many of our children.

21.   Pinpointing specific admission criteria was critical to the smooth functioning of the school. The student and his or her parenting adult(s) must agree to work under a contract on specific social and academic goals as set up by a multidisciplinary team. Students with problems too great for the school to deal with, such as schizophrenia or other mental disorders, need to be assigned to a more intensive environment equipped to meet those specific conditions. There was always pressure on CAL to enroll a greater number of students than the staff felt it was capable of assisting. This produced tension between the CAL administration and the public schools. The admissions criteria helped to reduce some of that tension.

22.   A transition process is usually best to insure that a student leaving CAL is able to transfer his successes achieved at the school into the public school setting. The receiving school needs to be fully informed of the student's progress to date and the kinds of support systems he needs to enhance the probability of his success at the new school

Tremendous pressures are placed on the public schools to provide services for many different kinds of youth. The schools do not have the resources to do all that is asked of them. Debates are ongoing as to how a school can use its fiscal resources more wisely. Needs seem endless. The model provided through the school for healing establishes the fact that we do know how to help many of our behaviorally maladjusted students. We also know that these young people are worth saving. They really are capable and caring human beings; and if they fail to develop into productive adults within our culture, we all lose individually and collectively. We lose the benefit of their insights; their creative talents; and, of course, their taxes. If we do not help them, then we receive their continued anger and the results of that anger. Society pays a price for failing to assist its young people. The cost is paid by the victims of that anger and by the taxpayers who pay for the justice system required to cope with their angry, desperate behavior. Society also pays into the next generations as it tries to compensate for the lack of appropriate parenting the unassisted, troubled youth, as adults, provide to their children. Our culture has become one in which an adult either contributes to it or takes away from it. This book can help us better understand what it is that we need to do to turn the lives of our troubled youth around, and it can give us the will to do what must be done to reach that goal.

REFERENCES

Bailey, R., & Morton, J. (1970). *RAID: A formula for positive classroom management.* Clearwater, FL: Pinellas County School System.

Carey, B. (1998, July 15). Boot camp fails to cut recidivism. *The Tennessean,* pp. A1–2.

Colon-Tarrats, N. I. (1988). *Cimarrones: A life history analysis of Puerto Rican dropouts in Boston.* Unpublished doctoral dissertation, Harvard University, Cambridge, MA.

Epstein, K. (1989). *Early school leaving: What the leavers say.* Unpublished doctoral dissertation, University of California, Berkeley.

Farrell, E. (1990). *Hanging in and dropping out: Voices of at-risk high school students.* New York: Teachers College Press.

Feuerstein, R. (1979). *The dynamic assessment of retarded performers.* Baltimore: University Park Press.

Fullan, M. (1994). *Change forces.* New York: Falmer.

Glasser, W. (1986). *Control theory in the classroom.* New York: Harper & Row.

Kershaw, M. A., & Blank, C. (1993, April). *Student and educator perceptions of the impact of an alternative school structure.* Paper presented at the American Education Research Association, Atlanta, GA.

Kennedy, R. L. 1993). *A study of four student pushouts from the perspective of four sociological theories.* Unpublished doctoral dissertation, University of Tennessee, Knoxville.

Kozol, J. (1992). *Savage inequalities.* New York, Crown Publisher.

Kronick, R., & Hargis, C. (1990). *Dropouts: Who drops out and why—and the recommended action.* Springfield, IL: Charles C. Thomas.

Lippman, W. (1922). *Public opinion.* New York: Macmillan.

Madsen, C. H., Jr., & Madsen, C. K. (1970). *Teaching/discipline—behavioral principles toward a positive approach.* Boston: Allyn & Bacon.

Merton, R. K. (1957). *Social theory and social structure.* Glencoe, IL: The Free Press.

Rowley, M. W. (1989). *An ethnographic inquiry into the reasons why students drop out of high school.* Unpublished doctoral dissertation, Brigham Young University, Provo, UT.

Schur, E. W. (1971). *Labeling deviant behavior.* New York: Harper & Row.

Sizer, T. (1992). *Horace's school: Redesigning the American high school.* Boston: Houghton Mifflin.

Spolin, V. (1986). *Theater games for the classroom: A teacher's handbook.* Chicago: Northwestern University Press.

Swadener, E. B. (1990). Children and families "at-risk": Etiology, critique, and alternative paradigms. *Educational Foundations, 4,* 17–39.

Trueba, H. T., & Spindler, G., & Spindler, L. (1989). *What do anthropologists have to say about dropouts?* New York: Falmer.

Woods, P. (1979). Ethnography and theory construction in educational research. In R. G. Burgess (Ed.), *The research process in educational settings: Ten case studies* (pp. 51-78). Lewes, UK: Falmer Press.

INDEX

Studies in the Postmodern Theory of Education

General Editors
Joe L. Kincheloe & Shirley R. Steinberg

Counterpoints publishes the most compelling and imaginative books being written in education today. Grounded on the theoretical advances in criticalism, feminism and postmodernism in the last two decades of the twentieth century, Counterpoints engages the meaning of these innovations in various forms of educational expression. Committed to the proposition that theoretical literature should be accessible to a variety of audiences, the series insists that its authors avoid esoteric and jargonistic languages that transform educational scholarship into an elite discourse for the initiated. Scholarly work matters only to the degree it affects consciousness and practice at multiple sites. Counterpoints' editorial policy is based on these principles and the ability of scholars to break new ground, to open new conversations, to go where educators have never gone before.

For additional information about this series or for the submission of manuscripts, please contact:

Joe L. Kincheloe & Shirley R. Steinberg
637 West Foster Avenue
State College, PA 16801